THE HIDDEN
TREASURE
OF LAMU

R H I N O 🦏 T A L E S

S H E L   A R E N S O N

THE HIDDEN TREASURE OF LAMU

Published by Multnomah Youth
a part of the Questar publishing family

© 1996 by Sheldon Arensen
International Standard Book Number: ISBN: 0-88070-900-6

Cover design: Kevin Keller
Cover illustration: Kenneth Spengler

Printed in the United States of America

For information:
QUESTAR PUBLISHERS, INC.
POST OFFICE BOX 1720
SISTERS, OREGON 97759

Library of Congress Cataloging-in-Publication Data

Arensen, Sheldon.
      The hidden treasure of Lamu / by Shel Arensen.
          p.   cm. — (Rhino tales)
      Summary: The members of the Rugendo Rhinos Club visit the island of Lamu,
in Kenya, where, after uncovering a smuggling ring, they are trapped and held
prisoner.
      ISBN 0-88070-900-6 (alk. paper)
      [1. Clubs — Fiction. 2. Robbers and outlaws — Fiction. 3. Christian life —
Fiction. 4. Kenya — Fiction. 5. Mystery and detective stories.] I. Title. II. Series.
PZ7.A683Hi   1996
[Fic] — dc20
                                                                            96-15675
                                                                            CIP
                                                                            AC

96 97 98 99 00 01 02 03 04 05 — 10 9 8 7 6 5 4 3 2 1

To my son, Reid, a budding silversmith who learned his trade
on the island of Lamu.

THE
RHINO HORN

"This meeting of the Rugendo Rhinos Club is now called to order," Matt announced. "Dean, you're the secretary, so take roll call."

I cleared my throat and looked down at my notebook. "Matt," I called.

"Of course I'm here!" Matt said with a snort. "I'm the one who told you to read the roll call. But you don't have to call my name."

"Sorry, Matt," I said. Matt Chadwick, the captain of our club, likes to run things his way.

I went on. "Dave."

"Here," answered Dave Krenden. He's our club engineer. I think he inherited his inventing and building skills from his father, a builder at our mission station called Rugendo, located in the central Kenyan highlands of Africa.

"Jon," I said.

"Here," said Jon. "Let's get this meeting over with so we can go hunting." Jon Freedman loves to hunt. We spend more time looking for things than actually shooting. With our air rifles we can't shoot anything bigger than birds anyway. But Jon loves to track animals. Jon's dad is the doctor at the Rugendo Mission Hospital.

"We're all here, Matt," I said.

"Good," said Matt. "Actually I know we're all here. But what good is a club if we don't have club rules? And one of those rules is taking roll. Okay, I called today's meeting because I think our clubhouse needs to be fixed up. And I don't just mean cleaning. I mean putting up some new decorations. Anyone have any animal skulls they want to donate?"

Jon liked that idea. "Yeah, we could hang a buffalo skull on the door."

"Anyone know where to find one?" Dave asked. But none of us knew about any spare buffalo heads.

"That's okay," said Dave. "A buffalo would probably be too heavy for the door of our tree house anyway."

"I have a baboon skull," I said. "The teeth look kind of fierce."

"A baboon skull!" Matt said. "No, thanks, Dean." I shut up pretty quickly. Having my idea rejected by Matt was like falling into an icy-cold trout stream in the Aberdare Mountains.

"If only we'd kept that genet cat we trapped that time the Dorobo hunter showed us the poison arrow tree," Jon said. "We could have put his skin up on the wall."

"Yeah," Matt laughed. "I can still see that cat squirming through the chicken wire and sprinting for the woods."

Dave had his index finger on his chin, scratching slowly. "Stand back for a great idea," I whispered. "Dave's thinking."

We all watched Dave. His eyes seemed to look through us. Then he turned and asked a question. "We're the Rugendo Rhinos, aren't we?"

"Of course we are!" Matt answered. "Get to the point, Dave."

Dave continued on his measured way. "Rhinos have horns, don't they?"

"Yes, yes, rhinos have horns," Matt said impatiently.

Dave looked at each of us. Finally he said, "Wouldn't it be great if we had a rhino horn on our door?"

"Oh, great," Matt groaned. "And where are we going to find a rhino horn? It's illegal to even have a horn these days with all the poaching going on in this country."

Dave held up his hand for silence. "I know we can't get a real horn. But we could make one."

"How?" I asked.

Dave dropped his idea on us. "We could cast one out of aluminum."

None of us said anything. We waited for Dave to explain.

"My dad was teaching me about metal casting just last week. He's got some new equipment in his shop and I'm sure he would help us. All we have to do is make a rhino horn out of plaster of Paris. Then we could use the plaster horn as the pattern. My dad puts green sand in a metal box called a flask—"

"Green sand?" interrupted Matt. "Where do we find green

sand? I've seen gray sand, white sand, brown sand, even black sand. But I've never seen green sand!"

"Green just means the sand is wet so it can hold the shape of the pattern," Dave explained. "Once the pattern is pushed into the sand in the flask, which is divided into two halves, we remove the plaster rhino horn. My dad pokes a hole in the sand called a sprue. Then we'll put the two halves of the flask back together."

"I'm getting a bit confused," Matt said, "but if you know what you're doing...."

"My dad does," Dave answered. "Anyway, finally we melt some aluminum and pour it into the sprue hole. The aluminum fills in the shape of the rhino horn in the sand. When it cools we take the sand off, and we have an aluminum rhino horn. We can file it down so it's smooth and hang it on our tree house door."

"That's good, Dave!" said Matt. "I really like that idea. We get a great trophy for our clubhouse. And we get to do something cool like melt aluminum?"

Dave nodded. "My dad has a special dish called a crucible," he said, "just to melt metal."

"How are we going to know what size to make our model horn?" Jon asked.

"My dad has some rhino pictures he took in Amboseli Game Park a few years ago," I said. "I bet we could use those to design it."

"Sounds great," Dave agreed. "I could figure out the size from the pictures."

Matt wanted to melt the aluminum right away. When Dave told him we had to plan things out first and melting the metal would be the last stage, Matt began to lose interest.

"You can be in charge of the project, Dave," Matt said. "Call us when it's time to pour the aluminum into the mold."

"It'll take several days," Dave said. "A rhino horn will be much easier than some other designs, but you can't expect it to be done today."

"Okay," Matt said. "Meeting's over. Let's go hunting."

"All right!" said Jon, clambering down the rope ladder. "I want to try some of those tracking skills the Dorobo hunter taught us during our adventure with the poison arrow tree."

"If you want an aluminum rhino horn, Matt," Dave said, "I'd better go home and start working on it."

"I'll go with you," I said. "I need to find those rhino pictures for you."

"All right, then," Matt said. "We'll check with you at your father's shop after our hunt. See you guys." Then he followed Jon into the forest.

Dave and I walked back to Rugendo. "Actually, I'm glad Matt won't be with us while we make the model," Dave said. "He's always in such a hurry we'd have done a sloppy job."

We went by my dad's office and asked him for his pictures of rhinos. He took us into the small darkroom set up for the magazine and found a couple of eight-by-ten prints. "Yeah, this one will do great," Dave said holding a print up to the light.

We went to his dad's workshop and Dave made some measurements and then drew a few sketches. I mostly watched and gave him the things he needed, like a nurse helping a surgeon. I had more patience than Jon or Matt, but I didn't think I was that great at art. I tried to draw a chameleon for art class the year before. Maybe I overdid it on the color changes because my teacher congratulated me on the beautiful picture of an African hoopoe, a kind of bird.

By late in the afternoon, Dave had cast the model horn of plaster of Paris. It was over a foot long and looked just like a rhino horn. Dave had even carved grooves in the model just like in the rhino pictures.

A little before supper Matt and Jon came in with stories of the monkeys they'd seen and the bushbucks they had tracked. "We even had a shot at a turaco, but he flew away so I must have missed," Jon said.

Dave's dad had just come home from work. Dave explained our project to him. His dad said he already had some sand prepared and could help us the next day.

We left Dave and walked home. After dropping Jon at his house, I saw my dad outside Matt's house talking with Matt's dad. They waved us over. "How would you two like to take a trip to Lamu?" Matt's dad asked.

"To Lamu?" Matt asked. "The island city off the northern coast of Kenya? The one where there are no cars and tiny narrow streets?"

His dad nodded. "We've just been talking about making a survey trip there to see if there's any way we can tell that city about Jesus. It's a strongly Muslim area and very little has been done. Anyway, we'll be making the trip in a few days. We'll probably be gone a little over a week. And we thought you boys would like to come."

"We'd love to," said Matt. "All right! A trip to Lamu!"

"What about the other Rhinos?" I asked. "Can they come, too?"

Our dads looked at each other. "Well, school's out right now," my dad said. "We have enough room in our Land

Rover if their parents say it's okay. We're going to drive as far as Malindi and then join a pastor who studied here at our Bible school. From there we'll travel to Lamu by bus."

"And can we stop at Amboseli on the way?" Matt asked. "Can we take an extra day and see some animals in the game park?"

Mr. Chadwick thought for a moment and then said, "Tell you what. If all four of you Rhinos are going, we'll try to make the trip more fun for you guys. I'll talk with Mr. Krenden and Dr. Freedman tomorrow. If they agree, then I'll give you our schedule."

"All right!" Matt said, hurling a pebble at the pepper tree in his front yard. "We get to take a trip to Lamu!"

ELEPHANTS AT AMBOSELI GAME PARK

We packed the last bit of our gear into the Land Rover in the foggy darkness before the dawn. I shivered, even wearing two T-shirts and a sweatshirt.

"That's it," Mr. Chadwick said. "Jump in, boys, and we'll be on our way." The Land Rover fired to life, belching out thick diesel smoke. Jon's and Dave's parents had agreed to let them come along. Matt's dad had added a few days to the trip just for us. First we'd stop over in Amboseli Game Park at the foot of Africa's tallest mountain, Mt. Kilimanjaro. Then we'd spend a night in Mombasa and visit Old Town while my dad and Matt's dad talked with missionaries there about Lamu.

Our third night would be at the Lutheran Guest House in Malindi before joining up with the Kenyan pastor in Malindi and catching a bus to Lamu.

As we huddled together in the back seat of the car — four of us where three should sit — Matt congratulated Dave on the rhino horn we had cast for our clubhouse up in the giant *mugumo* tree.

"It came out pretty well," Dave agreed.

Matt's eyes sparkled. "I really liked the part where your dad helped us pour the melted metal. And I couldn't believe how realistic it looked after we took it out of the sand."

"Well," Dave said, more into perfection than Matt, "it will still take some more work, filing off some of the rough edges. But I think it will look great."

"You're going to be a *fundi,* just like your dad," I said. *Fundi* means carpenter here in Kenya.

Dave smiled. "I like creating things. After I work on a project, it makes me feel good to know I did a good job."

The sun began pinking the horizon and soon popped up like a giant frisbee. The warm rays chased away the pockets of fog. We stopped in Nairobi at an Esso station to get diesel fuel. While the men filled the Land Rover, we ran to a nearby stand and bought some *mandazi* — square Kenyan dough-nuts. The owner wrapped them in a sheet of newspaper which soaked up the excess grease.

We drove through Nairobi, narrowly avoiding a honking *matatu* at a traffic roundabout. The *matatu,* a minibus designed to carry twenty-five passengers, groaned and sagged under the mass of people that had squeezed in. The turn-boy, or fare collector, hung onto the ladder on the side of the bus calling for passengers. "Buruburu, Buruburu," he kept shouting, indicating the area of Nairobi the *matatu* was headed for. Then he slapped the side of the brightly painted bus with his hand and the driver slammed on his brakes to let out a passenger. My dad pointed at the sign painted on the back of the bus as he swerved to avoid the vehicle. "God help us!" the sign read.

"Whenever I see a *matatu* driver driving like that I pray that God will help all the passengers to reach their destination safely," my dad said.

"I saw one last week that had the Los Angeles Lakers team logo painted on it," said Matt. As we passed through the city we had a contest to find which *matatu* had the funniest name. We saw several vehicles proclaiming: "Soul Winning Tours and Safaris." The funniest one was an old green pickup with a sign above the cab saying: "No hurry in Africa," because he drove so fast we couldn't catch up with him.

Soon we'd passed through the bustling center of Nairobi and turned south at Athi River. We drove through a dry thornbush-infested landscape and saw a few Maasai herding cattle. Finally, hot and thirsty, we arrived at Namanga, the border town between Kenya and Tanzania. After filling the fuel tank again we stepped into a small cafe. Flies scattered off the table where we sat down. A waiter gave us a red plastic-backed menu with a photocopied page stuck in the middle beneath a clear plastic sheet. Half the items had been crossed off with ballpoint pen.

"Do you have steak and chips?" Mr. Chadwick asked, pointing at the menu.

The waiter shook his head. "Sorry," he said. "We are out of steak."

"What about just chips?" Matt asked.

The waiter shook his head.

My dad asked, "What do you have that is ready to serve?"

The waiter looked relieved. "We have rice and stew."

We ordered for six and asked for Cokes. "*Leta barafu,*" Matt asked, wanting ice with his Coke.

"Sorry," the waiter said. "No ice." But he brought the Cokes right away with a straw in each bottle. Even though the sodas weren't cold, at least they were wet. Soon he served us plates heaped with rice and a steaming bowl of beef stew to be spooned like gravy over the rice. It was delicious.

After paying for the meal and tipping the waiter, my dad asked him if he liked to read. When he said he did, Dad sent me to the car to bring a couple of copies of the Christian magazine he edited. The man was elated. Even the cook came out of the kitchen when he heard there were magazines. "*Wapi yangu?*" he asked. "Where's mine?" I ran and got a few more for him. Both were sitting at a table reading before we left.

After Namanga we got onto a dirt track heading for the game park. My dad pointed to a tower of clouds ahead. "That's Mt. Kilimanjaro," he said. "We might get a glimpse of it tonight. If not, we should see it early in the morning. But during the day it's usually covered with clouds."

After about an hour, Jon had to go to the bathroom. We asked my dad to stop so we could use the bushes. We had scattered to various bushes when Matt suddenly screamed. He came rushing back to the car. "What's wrong?" I asked.

"Something big—" he started and pointed back over his shoulder. We looked and saw the head of a giraffe sticking up over a thorn tree. Its large brown eyes looked at us curiously, then it reached out its long black tongue and tore off a mouthful of leaves and thorns before moving along in a graceful walk.

Jon laughed first. "You're scared of a giraffe?" he asked.

Matt was annoyed. "No, of course not," he said. "I was just looking down and suddenly I saw something big and brown moving in the tree in front of me. I ran back here. I wasn't scared of a giraffe. I was just scared of some big brown thing."

"You don't have to defend yourself," Matt's dad said, putting an arm on his shoulder. "Any of us would have jumped if a giraffe started spying on us. Now, let's get going."

After a hot, dusty drive we saw the gate for Amboseli Game Park. We paid the park fees, got directions for the campsite and left some magazines with the rangers before driving into the park. As we drove along we came to a large dry lake bed. Two young impala bucks practiced battling each other. We could hear the crack as their horns met. White dust kicked up under their hooves.

We saw the gray shapes of elephants under the acacia trees. They flapped their ears gently to keep cool. But they wouldn't come out in the open. "We might as well go set up camp," my dad said. "It's too hot for most of the animals. We'll take a game drive in the late afternoon."

We found the campsite and set up our tents. Then we laid out our thin camping mattresses under an acacia tree and tried to cool off. At 4 P.M. the men turned on the pressure stove and boiled some water for tea. Matt's dad opened a tin of homemade cookies.

Later we drove around the park looking at animals. The elephants had come out from under the trees. We saw one baby elephant playing around, running back and forth. But whenever he wandered too far from the herd, a mother elephant would rush over and give him a firm swat with her trunk.

"We'd like to see a rhino," Matt said. "After all, we are the Rugendo Rhinos."

"We might get lucky," his dad said. "I read that they recently released a young rhino here in the park. He's called Morani. His parents were killed by poachers. He was rescued and then raised in the Nairobi Animal Orphanage. But even though they've released him to the wild, he's too scared to go far. Usually he hangs around the lodge where all the tourists stay."

"Well, let's drive by the lodge," Matt urged.

As we neared the lodge we saw something big and gray in the grass. The gray mass started to move. It was a rhino! When it saw our car, it came running, almost like a playful dog. My dad took a few pictures as the rhino posed for us.

"There used to be a lot of rhinos in this park," my dad said. "But poaching has wiped out many of them. Morani here will be lucky to avoid the same fate, especially since he's so friendly to humans."

We drove to the acacia forest, hoping to see a leopard in the trees, but we found none.

On the way back to camp we saw a small pride of lions.

"I want to see a lion make a kill," Jon said.

But these lions looked rather full and lazy. One mother had two cubs that kept pouncing on her, swatting at her and biting on her tail. The lioness snarled in warning and then, when the cubs got too pesky, she'd send them tumbling with her paw. We watched until it began to grow dark, and then drove to camp.

As we gathered some firewood for our campfire, we could see Mt. Kilimanjaro peeking out from its skirt of ragged clouds. "Wow! Look at that mountain," Dave said in awe.

"Over 18,000 feet high at the top," I said. For once my ability to memorize facts and figures came in handy.

After roasting skewers of marinated meat over the fire and baking potatoes in the coals, we ate supper under the stars. A few hyenas wailed mournfully in the distance and a lion grunted somewhere over the hill.

We sang songs and prayed before we headed for bed. All four of us Rhinos laid out our sleeping bags in the old canvas tent and zipped down the mosquito net. We told jokes and stories for awhile, then drifted off to sleep.

Suddenly I woke up. Our tent was moving! I found myself tumbled against Matt, who also woke up.

"Why are you climbing all over me, Dean?" he asked grumpily.

"I'm not!" I said. "Our tent is moving!"

chapter three

FORT JESUS

We began to scream as we tumbled into each other. The tent jerked crazily first one way, then another. We felt like someone was swinging our tent like a giant pillow in a pillow fight.

"Help! Help!" Matt shouted.

We heard our dads outside and I could see a flashlight beam. "Go on! Get out of here!" I heard my dad yell.

"He's stuck," Matt's dad said. "The rope is tangled around his leg. Grab a *panga* knife and we'll cut it."

Silence. Then a few more jerks. Then, "Here's the knife. Watch out. Don't let him step on you! There."

The tent stopped moving. We lay huddled together in a tangle of sleeping bags and pillows, our tent caved in on top of us like a mosquito net that's fallen off its hook.

My dad's voice penetrated the canvas. "Are you boys all right?"

"We're okay dad," I answered. "Just scared. What's going on?"

Mr. Chadwick and my dad burrowed in through the folds of the tent and released us. "Thank God you're all right," Matt's dad said, giving him a big hug.

"What happened?" Matt asked.

"An elephant got caught on one of the ropes to your tent," my dad explained. "We heard him rustling through our garbage dump a while ago. In fact, we watched him through our tent window for a while and thought of waking you guys up. Then the elephant walked away. Most animals see a tent as a solid object, so we weren't worried about him trying to step on you as you slept. But he came too close to the ropes of your tent and got one leg tangled. Then he started running away. We saw your tent collapse and he started pulling you. We were afraid the elephant might panic and trample you."

"So you cut the rope off his leg?" Matt asked. "How'd you get so close to him without getting hurt?"

"Actually I cut the rope off right at the tent," Matt's dad answered. You never realize how big an elephant is until you see one up close."

"Well," my dad said, "let's thank the Lord you guys are safe. Then we can set up your tent again and we'll pray nothing else happens tonight."

When the tent was back up we spread our sleeping bags out again. At first we were too excited to fall asleep.

"Man, what a great story this will be back at school," Matt said. "We were dragged around by a mad elephant!"

"It wasn't a mad elephant," corrected Dave, "just a scared one."

"I'm going to write to my grandma back in America about this," I said.

"I don't think my grandmother would be too happy to hear about it," said Jon. "She's already worried because Africa is full of bugs. My mom wants her to visit. If she hears about an elephant carrying us along in our tent I don't think she'd ever come!"

We finally drifted off. But I woke up several times sweating and thinking an elephant had just trampled me. I had to ask God to take away my bad dreams.

We woke up early the next day. Jon ran around looking at all the elephant tracks near our tent. My dad took a few pictures. Then we ate oatmeal for breakfast, looking at the snow-capped Kibo peak of Mt. Kilimanjaro.

Matt looked up at the mountain. "Someday I'm going to climb to the top," he said.

"Maybe in a couple of years," his dad answered.

We drove out of the park and over bumpy roads for most of the morning before finally coming back to the main road to Mombasa.

By the time we had crossed onto Mombasa Island, we were drenched with sweat because it was so hot. Our dads stopped to visit some missionaries. We drank some iced tea to cool off. Then my dad asked if we'd like to see Fort Jesus while they visited.

"Fort Jesus?" asked Jon. "What's that? Some kind of church?"

"No," my dad answered. "Fort Jesus was built by the

Portuguese on the corner of the island in 1593 to protect the harbor. Now it's been turned into a museum."

He drove us to the edge of Old Town. We got out next to a large cannon on wheels. "Boy, this sure is a modern cannon for being almost four hundred years old," Dave commented.

My dad laughed. "The British captured that cannon from the Germans in World War I. But you'll see some old Portuguese cannons as well as piles of cannon balls inside the fort." He gave us money for tickets and Cokes and waved good-bye.

We walked up the stone ramp through the wide open wooden doors. There were Portuguese words inscribed on the plastered walls that told some of the fort's history. We didn't know Portuguese, but a little white sign on the wall was in English. Once inside, we walked up the stairs and looked down over the Indian Ocean through small slits cut out for muskets.

Other signs told of the great battle of Fort Jesus. The Portuguese held out for thirty-three months against Omani Arabs who had ruled there before the Portuguese had taken control. By the end of the siege only a handful of Portuguese were left alive in Fort Jesus. The rest starved to death or died of diseases like the plague. We saw piles of rusty cannon balls in the fort's courtyard.

"This place is great!" Matt said. "If there weren't so many tourists around we could play Portuguese and Arabs. There are some cool hiding places in these rooms." We looked into a room of crumbling coral through a small window with rusting iron bars.

I was fascinated by a display in the small museum. There were coins, pots and other things from an old galleon that had sunk in the harbor right in front of Fort Jesus. A small bulletin board said archaeologists had discovered the ship and showed pictures of them diving in scuba gear. "That's what I'd like to learn how to do," I said to Dave. "Scuba diving."

Dave liked the antique Arab jewelry, displayed in a glass case. "Look at these silver necklaces," Dave said. "You can tell they were cast. But the designs are much smaller, with a lot more details than the work we did with the rhino horn. I wonder what they used for forms back then?"

"Who cares," Matt said, wandering out of the museum. "I'm hot. Let's go find something to drink."

We walked out of Fort Jesus and found a man selling sodas by the entrance. As we swigged down our drinks, we looked back up at the massive gray walls of the fort. "Now what?" Matt asked. "Your dad's not coming back for a while and I don't want to sit around waiting for him." He turned and looked across the street. Narrow roads disappeared into an area of Mombasa called Old Town. One sign invited people to a curio store. Matt's eyes lit up. "Let's go for a walk through Old Town."

"Do you know the way?" I asked cautiously.

"No, but who could get lost?" Matt answered. "We'll find a road leading back."

"Yeah," Jon agreed. "If we can find our way through the forest around Rugendo, I'm sure we can find our way through Old Town."

I looked at Dave. He shrugged and we followed the other two who were already moving down the narrowing streets. We passed by several Muslim churches called mosques and soon the stench of fish began to overpower us.

A sign told us we had reached the old harbor. A few Arab dhows, wooden sailing ships, were anchored taking on cargo for the Arabian Peninsula. A large fish exporter had a warehouse next to the harbor. We watched for a few minutes and then made our way into Old Town. Small wooden verandas leaned out of many second-story homes with clothes laid out to dry on the wooden slats. A scarred cat with one ear hissed and leaped behind a pile of garbage. A car hooted behind us and we had to lean against a wall to allow the vehicle to pass.

"I wonder if Lamu will be like this?" I asked.

"It's supposed to have even narrower streets. But Lamu has no cars, remember?" Dave said.

As we turned a corner we saw a sign for a silversmith. "Hey, look at that," Dave said, grabbing me. "Let's go in." He pulled me in with him. Matt and Jon walked farther into Old Town without us.

Inside the silversmith's shop an old Arab man stood behind a glass display case filled with silver jewelry — rings, bracelets, necklaces, earrings, small charms. A younger man sat twisting some silver wire near the back of the dimly lit room.

"What can I do for you, gentlemen?" the man behind the counter asked.

"Well," Dave began, "I'm really interested in how you cast silver. I've never done it before, but we made a rhino horn out of aluminum and—"

"You wish to be a silversmith," the man said in a whispery kind of voice. He took us past his assistant and into a small workshop. He began to explain how he made models of small animals or other objects. He said he pressed the model into the soft chalky bottom of a cuttlefish bone, leaving an impression of one side of the object. Then he would press another cuttlefish bone against the half-exposed model until the two bones met. After this he would take them apart and remove the model, leaving an impression in the bones.

"So you use cuttlefish bones for your forms?" Dave asked, amazed.

The man nodded and explained how he tied the two bones together. Then he heated the silver, mostly old coins and outdated jewelry that he bought. He poured the hot silver into the mold. When the metal cooled, he opened the cuttlefish and he had his silver elephant, leopard or any of the other different objects he could make.

"That's great," Dave said. "I'll bet we could do that."

"I don't know about the silver part," I said, "but I do know where we can collect cuttlefish bones for forms. They get carried in on the tide and we can find them up along the high water mark under the dried out seaweed."

The man smiled. "Yes, you could learn. But you must be taught. Do you want me to teach you?"

Dave's eyes sparkled. "I'd love to." Then his shoulders sagged. "But we're leaving tomorrow. We're on our way to Lamu."

"Lamu," the man said. "Even better. I have a cousin in Lamu. We learned silversmithing together in Yemen from an uncle who is a master silversmith. My cousin sometimes takes people on and teaches them the basics of working with silver."

"Do you think he could really teach me?" Dave asked.

"As long as you pay for the silver you use," he answered. "It won't be hard to find my cousin. He has a shop on the main street in Lamu. Just ask for Omari the silversmith."

As we walked out of the shop, Dave couldn't keep the big smile off his face. "Man, I'll be able to learn how to be a silversmith in Lamu. I can't wait. Maybe I can make some of those fancy necklaces like we saw in the museum today."

"Don't get carried away," I said. But his happiness was catching.

"I wonder how far ahead Matt and Jon are by now?" I asked as we hurried down the street, now gloomy with late afternoon shadows. We took a turn. Then another. Then a third. The ribbon-thin road ended at a wall.

"I don't think we'll find those two guys," Dave said. "We'd better just head back to Fort Jesus and wait for them there."

We walked a bit more slowly. At a crossroads I started to turn right. "No, it's this way," Dave said, pulling me to the left.

"Are you sure?" I asked, following him. After another minute and two more turns, Dave said, "Maybe you were right, Dean. This doesn't look familiar."

We tried to make our way back but everything looked different. Finally we leaned against a wall. I looked at Dave, trying to swallow my growing panic. "I hate to admit it, but I think we're lost."

THE RUINS
OF GEDI

My stomach tightened like my slingshot when I stretched
it back to shoot at a bird. I felt like throwing up. Dave didn't
look too good either.

Looking at me, he said, "Which way, friend?"

"I don't know. Maybe we'd better pray."

So right there in the shadow of a mosque we asked God
to show us the way out of the tangled maze of streets.

As we opened our eyes, we saw two Somali men walking
toward us, their white *kanzu* robes swaying in the breeze.
Dave asked them in Swahili which road led to Fort Jesus.
Both men looked puzzled and one answered with words that
seemed to be formed way in the back of his throat. We didn't

understand Somali and they must not have known any Swahili. They kept walking up the street.

Just then a gust of wind brought with it the scent of fish. "The fish market must be up this way," Dave said, trotting off quickly. Following our noses, we found our way back to the harbor and saw the street that led back to Fort Jesus.

We were almost running by the time we reached the fort. My dad stood there, leaning on the hood of the car. Matt and Jon sat on the wall nearby.

"Where have you two been?" My dad looked upset. "Matt and Jon said you ditched them in Old Town."

"It was my fault," Dave said, telling how he'd pulled me into the silversmith's shop and then how we had lost our way coming back.

I looked up at him. "We were scared, Dad. I know it sounds silly, but we weren't sure which way to turn. All the streets twisted and turned. So we stopped and prayed."

"And the smell of fish led us home," Dave said, laughing.

My dad smiled. "Well, I guess we'd better thank the Lord you're both back safely. The streets in Old Town can be very confusing."

After a short prayer, we jumped into the Land Rover. Matt whispered that he was sorry for almost landing us in trouble with my dad. "I thought you two were playing some sort of goofy hide and seek game with us," he said.

We spent the night with the missionaries there in Mombasa. After supper, while our dads went on talking, we went outside and tried to hit fruit bats out of a massive mango tree. We started by throwing rocks. As each rock hit the tree, bats erupted like flies off road-kill. The bats squeaked and flew around the tree in big looping arcs, whizzing by our ears. They used their sonar to know what was coming, so we couldn't hit any.

Then Matt had an idea. "I wonder if they have a tennis racket in the house," he said and ran in to ask. He came out a few minutes later, swinging a battered old wooden tennis racket. A couple of the frayed catgut strings had snapped. "Now," said Matt, "I know how to get one. You guys throw some rocks into the tree and as the bats fly around, I'll hit one with the tennis racket."

We tried it. The rocks stirred up another wild flurry of bats. Matt swung the tennis racket and a soft whump told us he'd connected.

"I hit one," Matt yelled. "I hit one. Help me find it."

We looked around in the dim moonlight. Jon found the bat underneath a frangipani tree. We gathered around. "Pick it up," Matt said.

"I'm not picking it up," I said.

"Me neither," Dave said, stepping back and shuddering.

"What about you, Jon?" Matt asked.

"No way," Jon said, shaking his head.

"What's the matter? Scared?" Matt taunted.

"No," said Jon. "But a bat bite could give me rabies."

The bat, recovering from its stunned state, crawled on the sandy ground, dragging itself along with its bent, leathery wings.

We all jumped back. "Wimps," Matt muttered in disgust. Then he reached out with the tennis racket and scooped the bat onto the strings. As he started to carry it to the porch light to get a better view, the pug-nosed creature pulled itself off the tennis racket and flew back to the mango tree.

Just then Matt's dad called us into the house. "You boys

better come in and get to bed," he said. "We're heading north tomorrow."

The next morning we drove across the Nyali Bridge and headed for Malindi. At Kilifi the long line of cars meant we'd have to wait a while for the ferry boat that carried cars across the channel.

"It won't be long before this ferry wait is a thing of the past here," my dad said. "Look over there."

We craned our heads out the window and saw the massive cement pillars in the middle of the channel.

"They're building a bridge," my dad said. "It's supposed to be finished by next year. Then all the cars will just drive across."

A honk behind us by an impatient tourist in a rental car made my dad realize the line of cars was moving forward. We inched ahead. But the ferry filled before we could get on. "We'll catch the next one," my dad said. "You boys might as well get out and try to catch some of the breeze. It's too hot to sit in the car."

We wandered over to a line of palm-thatched shelters by the side of the road. Vendors sold fruit, drinks, and assorted Kenyan souvenirs. A loud group of tourists scrambled out of a zebra-striped minivan and began looking at souvenirs. One man with a round belly and a bad sunburn haggled with a Kenyan boy over the price of a model of an outrigger canoe with orange sails. He must have thought if he shouted louder than the Kenyan boy, he'd get a better price. The Kenyan just smiled, sweat dripping off his forehead in the hot morning sun. He named a very high price. The tourist refused and made an offer at half the price. Reluctantly, the boy dropped his price a little at a time until the tourist was sure he'd gotten an outstanding bargain. He didn't know he'd still paid three times the normal price of the boat. But both the seller and the buyer were happy with the deal.

Matt laughed and whispered to us, "Tourists make such fools of themselves."

We walked over to where a man had a cart full of pine-apples. He had cut some of them up into long chunks. We each bought two and the man gave us wooden skewers. We stabbed the pieces we wanted and walked away eating the sweet, juicy fruit. We could see the ferry returning so we got back into the car.

As we did, Matt's dad turned around and said, "We're making good time. Would you boys like to stop off at the ruins of the old Arab town of Gedi? It's pretty close to the main road."

"We'd love to," Matt answered for all of us. "What's Gedi?"

My dad explained. "It's an old Arab city that was mysteri-ously abandoned around the sixteenth or seventeenth century. Archaeologists did a lot of digging so the main area is all opened up. Some of the ruins are still covered with thick growth and trees. But there are things to see, like a pillar tomb and some arched doorways. We'll get there about mid-day and have a picnic in the shade instead of in this baking hot Land Rover."

We drove onto the ferry. After the short crossing we drove up the steep ramp on the north side of the Kilifi channel, doing our best to avoid crowds of walk-on passengers who poured off the ferry in front of honking cars. An hour later, my dad swung the Land Rover onto the road leading to Watamu. Big signs announced a number of big hotels a few miles ahead, including one that specialized in taking people on deep sea fishing trips for sailfish. We turned off on a small sandy road. A sign with peeling green paint pointed the way to the Gedi ruins.

We parked under some trees and my dad bought tickets at the small office. A vervet monkey scampered across the path. One of the Kenyan wardens chased it away. The monkey sat in a tree and chattered back at him.

My dad bought a guidebook and we walked past an arched gate with large tree roots draped over it. The palace was the main section that had been dug up by archaeologists. Nearby stood a large building with a special room for visitors. Inside we saw a special tomb with a tall carved, coral pillar set on top. There were small sinks for hand washing as well as an old mosque with a special carved nook for holding the Koran, the holy book of Islam.

My dad read from the guidebook. "It says this town of Gedi was probably founded in the 1300s by wealthy Arabs. It prospered until sometime in the 1600s when it was abandoned. No one is sure why, but the likely reason is lack of water. Hey, this is interesting — the Africans who lived around here, mostly Giriama, believed Gedi was haunted by ghosts and refused to come here. Earlier in this century British people came to check out the ruins and they camped right here. But they said they could hardly sleep at night because they heard strange sounds."

"Ghosts?" Matt said. "Get real."

"Well, I don't know about ghosts," Matt's dad said, "but we do know that Satan has demonic forces that have power. Remember what happened to Jon and Kamau when the witch doctor put a curse on them?" I shuddered, remembering how Jon had almost died that time.

We all nodded. Matt's dad went on. "Well, the coastal area is known for some very powerful evil spirits called *djinn*. That's where the English word *genie* comes from. After seeing the "Aladdin" video, you kids may think a genie is only a make-believe character. But the *djinn* spirits are very powerful. Only Jesus Christ has power over them. I think the ghost stories of Gedi were accurate, except that the ghosts were probably *djinn* spirits, not comic book spooks."

We calmed down after Mr. Chadwick reminded us that God is stronger than *djinn* spirits. My dad took out his camera. "I've got to get some pictures of this place." His camera clicked as we posed in arched doorways and poked our heads out windows. When he was done, he said, "Let's have our picnic."

"It's hot here, Dad," I said.

"Then let's hike around the outside of the ruins. There are a lot more trees and it should be cooler in the shade."

We followed the path that led along the town wall. Mostly we could see crumbled piles of coral rock where the wall had been. In a few places, it had been glued together with cement. A large pile of rocks grabbed our attention. "What's that, Dad?" I asked.

"Probably a house that hasn't been explored," he answered.

"Really?" Jon said, excited. "Can we go dig and search for things? Maybe we'll find some treasure."

"I'm afraid not," my dad said. "The rules are to stay on the path and not to touch anything. Maybe someday another archaeologist will dig up some more of the town. For now, it's meant to be left alone."

We came to a cool place where a tamarind tree shaded a corner of the wall. "Let's eat here," Matt's dad said.

As we set out the sandwiches and drinks, my dad reached down and picked up a pod-like fruit that had fallen from the tamarind tree. "Anyone thirsty?" he asked. We all looked at him. "Try eating one of these," he said, taking a bite and sucking on the stringy fruit. His eyes closed and he winced. "Whew, a bit more sour than I expected." We all picked up some fruit and sucked on it. It had a sour taste, somewhere between a strong lemon and an orange.

We sat down and passed around the sandwiches. We'd also brought along some small finger bananas.

After everyone was served, Matt's dad gave thanks for the meal. After the prayer, Matt reached down for his sandwich and banana. "Hey," he said in an angry bellow, "someone swiped my lunch. Come on, who was it?"

When we'd persuaded him that none of us had taken his sandwich and banana, Matt said, "Well, it's gone. If you guys didn't hide it, who did?" Suddenly he turned pale. "Dad," he asked, "do those *djinn* spirits ever steal food?"

VASCO
DA GAMA'S
CROSS

"You don't think any ghosts are hanging around right now?" Matt went on. A small breeze rustled the leaves and I began to feel creepy, too.

Mr. Chadwick said, "I really don't think so. But in my experience, it's best to pray first." He bowed his head. "Lord, we don't know if there are evil spirits here, but we claim protection against them in the name of Jesus Christ."

He stopped abruptly when a banana peel landed on his head. We all looked up and saw a vervet monkey chewing the banana with his mouth open. He held Matt's sandwich in his hand.

Matt's dad laughed. "Well, that sure was a quick answer to prayer," he said. "Looks like the thief this time is a monkey, not *djinn* spirits."

Matt stood up. "That monkey stole my food!" he shouted, grabbing a stick and throwing it at the light-gray vervet. The furry bandit leaped higher into the tree with the sandwich in his mouth.

"That sandwich is gone, Matt," his dad said, chuckling. "Here, I'll give you mine."

After lunch we drove on to Malindi where we checked into the Lutheran Guest House. Our dads said it was okay to explore the town while they met with Samuel, the Kenyan pastor who would be traveling to Lamu with us.

We wandered through the town of Malindi, all the way to the end of the jetty where a rusty old boat was taking on cargo. "What's that over there?" Jon asked. He pointed to a white pillar sitting on a rocky outcrop at one end of the harbor.

An old Swahili man stood near us, throwing a fishing line into the water. He said, "That is Vasco da Gama's cross."

"Who was Vasco da Gama?" Matt asked.

"He was a Portuguese explorer who came to Malindi in 1498 after Columbus made his trip to America," I answered.

"That's right," the old man said. "Vasco da Gama came here on his way to the East Indies looking for a new trade route for bringing spices to Europe. When he came, he placed a small cross carved out of coral, to claim this land for Portugal and," he stopped to spit, "for Jesus Christ."

He looked angry. I tried to change the subject. "You said the cross was small. But that pillar looks huge."

"Yes," the man answered, "the pillar is large. The cross is

only the small thing at the top of it. The cross was originally much closer to town. But the Muslim leaders didn't want the symbol of the cross so close to our mosques. So this pillar was built and the cross was set on top. You boys should go see it. There's a path that goes out over the coral."

He pointed us in the right direction and we hiked over to see the cross up close. On the way we passed the crumbling ruins of the chapel that Vasco da Gama had built to bring Christianity to the African coast. It had served the few Portuguese soldiers who stayed on after his ships left the harbor.

At the pillar we looked up and saw the coral cross, about a foot tall. It had a Portuguese coat-of-arms on the side. "Whoa," I said. "It's almost 500 years old."

We told our dads about the cross that evening at supper and my dad told us some more of the history of the coast.

The next morning we got up early to catch the 6 A.M. bus to Lamu. Pastor Samuel met us at the bus station next to the fresh fruit market. We threw our bags in storage bays along the side of the bus under the windows and then pushed our way onto the bus. We actually had seat numbers, but when Dave and I found our seats, two ladies, wearing black dresses called *buibuis* that covered everything but their eyes, sat stoutly on the seats and refused to budge.

"Dad," I hissed, leaning to where he'd squeezed himself in between Matt's dad and Pastor Samuel, "these ladies are in our seats and we can't get them to move."

Pastor Samuel said he'd talk with them. They told him they had tickets but they didn't like sitting at the back of the bus where they'd been assigned seats. Sitting near the back made them feel sick, they said. So they had chosen better seats.

"We could force them to leave by calling the conductor," Pastor Samuel said. "Or we could follow our Lord's example and be servants by taking the seats assigned to the ladies at the back."

"No big deal to me," Dave said.

"I guess it's all right," I said. I often got carsick so I wasn't so sure how I'd do in the back of a swaying bus.

Pastor Samuel found the ladies' seat numbers and helped us move to the back. Our seats did have a window, but were right on top of the wheel well. A big hump filled the space where our feet should have gone.

"We're right on top of the back wheel," I said. "We'll get bumped around a lot."

"Just think of it as a Disneyland ride," Dave said. "Do you know how much people pay to go on those bumpy rides? We can have our own private adventure."

Matt and Jon sat a couple of rows ahead of us. People kept pushing onto the bus including several tourists dressed in shorts, sandals and faded tank tops. Soon every spot was filled. Then the stand-up passengers got on. They paid less, but they had to stand up for the six-hour trip. One of the men standing in the aisle looked down at Matt's and Jon's double seat. Since there was a small gap between Jon and the edge of the seat, the man in the aisle sat down. Before Jon could react, the man knocked Jon closer to Matt. He smiled and settled comfortably into most of Jon's seat.

"Hey, what's going on?" Jon asked. The man just smiled and looked straight ahead, ignoring Jon's protest.

Dave looked at me. "Looks like we should be thankful,"

he said. "At least no one is pushing to take up our space."
Just to be sure, I moved closer to the edge of the seat and
wedged my knees against the seat in front of me.

When the bus finally was loaded, the driver honked his
horn and drove onto the main street. Near the edge of town,
the bus stopped and all the standing passengers jumped out
and began running down the road.

"What's going on?" I asked Dave.

"I don't know," he answered.

Soon we came to a police roadblock. An officer leaned in
and counted heads to be sure the bus wasn't overloaded.

"I think I know why all those people got off," I said. "The
bus is only licensed to carry as many passengers as there are
seats."

The policemen motioned the bus to move on and the driver roared down the road before stopping around a corner.
Within five minutes the passengers who had jumped off
began filtering back onto the bus. I noticed that Jon had
traded places with Matt. With Matt on the aisle seat, no one
squeezed in next to them.

The bus began to pick up speed on the sandy road. Near
Mambrui we saw the ocean. After that we passed the salt-
works near Ngomeni, where large mounds of gray sea salt
had been reclaimed from ocean water.

"Look what's ahead," Dave said.

I looked out the window and saw some Somali men leading a herd of camels down the road.

"Maybe they're escaping from the war in their country," I
said.

Every once in a while the bus hit a hole in the road, send-
ing Dave and me into the air. By looking out the window and

taking deep sniffs of the outside air, I managed to keep from being sick. And, like Dave had said, if I thought of it as an amusement park ride, it was more fun.

The bus stopped before crossing a bridge over the Tana River. Two Kenyan soldiers wearing green combat fatigues and hoisting automatic rifles boarded the bus. They leaned against the open door.

"Those guys are our military escorts," I told Dave. "My dad told me that sometimes buses in this area are held up by *shifta,* or bandits. Things have gotten worse with all the fighting in Somalia. He said a number of armed Somalis have moved across the border into Kenya."

We drove down a smooth section of paved road that had been built over the swampy edges of the Tana River delta. The road was raised high above the wet grassy land around us. Doum palm trees grew in clusters. I saw something black moving behind some bushes. "Look over there, Dave," I said, pointing. "Buffalo."

We watched the herd of buffalo wallowing in the mud. Soon we saw large herds of topi, a chocolate-brown antelope with liver-colored marks on its back. They scattered at the sight of the bus. The bus began to rattle again as the pavement ended and we drove over gravel.

Suddenly we heard the driver shout, *"Shifta!"* The bus skidded on the loose surface as he braked to a stop.

My dad turned in his seat. "Get your heads down, boys! And pray!"

AMBUSH!

Before I ducked down in my seat, I saw the two Kenyan soldiers jump off the bus and land on their stomachs on the road. We heard the *shifta* leader tell the bus driver to order everyone out of the bus to be searched for valuables.

I closed my eyes and asked God to help us. Then I heard a loud popping noise. It seemed to be coming from under the bus.

Dave hit me on the shoulder. "Someone is shooting," he said.

The bus engine roared loudly and the bus lurched forward and began to pick up speed. I still had my hands clasped behind my head, trying to protect myself. But I looked up to try to figure out what was happening. I saw a blur of motion on the window to the right of us. Then I saw a black hand.

"Watch out!" I shouted to Dave. "Someone's coming in the window!"

"It's okay," Dave said. "He's one of the Kenyan soldiers."

He swung in the window followed by his fellow soldier. *"Endelea na upesi,* Keep going fast," he shouted up at the bus driver. The bus swayed from side to side as the driver sped away. The soldiers pushed their way up to the open door of the bus and looked back. The small band of *shifta* had disappeared into the bush.

Passengers shouted. Women wailed. One of the soldiers told everyone to be quiet. He asked if anyone was hurt. One man said his wife had died, but when the soldier took a quick look at her he said she'd only fainted. Then he explained what had happened. The soldiers had crawled under the bus while the *shifta* were making their demands. They had shot at the legs of the bandit closest to the bus driver. As he had fallen over, the driver had driven away as fast as possible. "We had to roll over quickly to catch the side of the bus," said the soldier, resting his weapon against his side. "We can be thankful no one was hurt. We will go quickly to Witu where we will report the attempted robbery. Security forces will chase the bandits down." The soldier adjusted his cap.

Pastor Samuel stood up and said he wanted to pray and thank God. Even though most of the passengers were Muslims, no one objected. As Samuel thanked God for our escape, a number of the passengers kept saying, *Allah kareem.* God is gracious.

The driver kept the bus going at top speed. Maybe it was the narrow escape. Or maybe it was the rolling motion as the bus hurtled over the sandy road. I asked Dave to swap places so I could stick my head out the window. The stiff breeze helped and I managed to keep my food in my stomach.

Soon we arrived at the small town of Witu. The soldiers jumped out of the bus and ran to the police station before the wheels stopped rolling. After a few shouts, one of the soldiers climbed on board a blue police Land Rover and it roared down the road.

A police officer and the other soldier talked with the bus driver, who told about his part in the escape from the bandits. The policeman told the bus to wait while he wrote down the report. Then the soldier would escort us the rest of the way.

Little boys had crowded around the bus holding up things to sell. Some held bananas. Others waved hard brown chunks of sugary candy. Still others shouted, "Simsim, simsim." They were selling sesame bars. Dave asked me to buy candy for him. So I reached out and bought candy and sesame bars.

"You want some?" Dave asked, chomping on the sweets.

My stomach did a flip. "No, I don't think so," I answered.

My dad turned around and asked if we were okay. We all nodded, although my stomach still churned.

"That could have been nasty back there," he said, and then turned back to stare out the bus window.

None of us wanted to talk about it. The bandits could have shot any one of us back there. I silently thanked God for keeping everyone safe.

Finally the soldier boarded the bus and we set out again. After an uneventful ride, the bus pulled up at a big sandy parking lot.

Everyone got off the bus. "Are we in Lamu now?" I asked my dad as I stretched my legs.

"No," he answered. "This is Mokowe. Lamu is that island over there." He pointed at a dense green swamp across a small channel. "The town of Lamu is on the northern part of that island. We'll have to catch a dhow ferry. So grab your bag and let's go."

We all wrestled our bags from the bus and walked to the dock. Two sweating men wearing ragged shorts grabbed our bags and threw them on top of a big pile on the dhow ferry boat. Then we were herded on board. All the seats around the edge had already been taken. We stood in the middle.

"What are we going to hold onto?" Dave asked. It turned out it didn't matter. Soon the deck was so full of people that we stood side by side like crayons in a box. We couldn't have fallen over if we'd tried.

The captain made sure the boat was full, and started up the old diesel engine. It coughed and gargled and then died. Muttering to himself, the captain and one of his sailors lifted up an old board and peered into the depths of the engine. The two men reached in and fiddled with something. Then they tried again. The engine burst into a thumping roar and the boat moved down the channel. We watched as the mangrove trees swept past. Soon we saw the rusty iron-sheeted roofs of houses in the distance. After about half an hour, the dhow pulled up at the dock.

"Well, boys," Matt's dad said. "We're here in Lamu."

We climbed off the boat. Right away, up the steps, young men and boys from Lamu rushed over and tried to carry our bags.

"Here," one of the men said to me. "I will be your guide." He tugged on my bag, but I pulled back.

"Dad," I called out. "All these guys are trying to be our guides."

My dad told the would-be guides that we already knew where we were going to stay.

"Where are you going?" one man asked. "I know the best places in Lamu."

"We're going to Lamu Guest House," my dad said.

"Lamu Guest House!" the man exclaimed. "I'll show you the way."

Despite my dad's protests that we didn't need a guide, this man refused to go away. "My name is Ali," he said. "You want to go for a dhow trip? I can arrange it. You like to fish? Swim? Just ask."

Dad couldn't help smiling. He leaned over to Mr. Chadwick and said in English, "I don't think this guy's going to give up." He let the pesky guide show us the way.

After a short walk we arrived at the Lamu Guest House on the Ndia Kuu, the main street of Lamu. The street was barely wide enough for four men side by side. And this was the main road.

We checked into the guest house. My dad didn't give any money to Ali, but did offer him a Christian magazine. Ali began to complain that he'd offered us such excellent directions he should be paid. But my dad just laughed and told him to be happy with the magazine. Ali grinned and went off. "Tomorrow I'll give you a tour of the city," he called.

"We don't need one!" my dad yelled back.

We went upstairs to our rooms. Above each bed a mosquito net was tied up in a large knot that dangled from a hook in the ceiling. The windows had rusty iron bars but no glass. Dave and I turned on the ceiling fan in our room, trying to get a breeze moving in the oven-like heat.

After we'd stashed our bags, my dad came in. "We're going to meet with some missionaries. So you boys will be free to look around. Lamu is a safe place. Just be careful not to step in any donkey droppings." He stopped and started to chuckle.

"What are you laughing at?" I asked.

"Well, since there are no cars in Lamu, anything heavy is carried by donkeys. And, of course, donkeys leave droppings. Last year the problem was so bad that they tried to enforce a new law requiring all donkeys to wear diapers. Can you believe it!"

"Donkey diapers!" laughed Matt, who had come in with Jon. "What a hoot!"

"Anyway," my dad went on, "watch your step and enjoy yourselves. We'll meet you later at the Olympic Restaurant. It's on the waterfront. I hear they serve the greatest lime milkshakes and excellent fresh fish. We'll see you boys when the sun goes down at six."

Matt led the way down the narrow streets of Lamu. We pushed our heads into a carpentry shop and watched men making carved two-piece chairs. As we walked on, Matt began to sniff. "I smell meat cooking," he said. Following his nose we came to a vendor roasting shish kebabs on a charcoal fire. The man used a barbecue made of old metal cans with holes in the bottom hammered together. *"Bei gani?* How much?" Matt asked. We each bought two sticks of meat and ate them as we walked.

"These are good," Matt said, "but they make me thirsty."

The spicy pepper sauce on the strips of meat left my lips burning, too. We found a Coca-Cola cart near the old fort that dominated the main square of Lamu. We sat on a cement bench as we drank our Cokes. Then we wandered deeper into the town. A sign hanging over the door of one small shop announced: Omari, Lamu Silversmith.

"Hey," Dave said, "this is the silversmith guy we heard about in Old Town in Mombasa. Let's go in." He disappeared into the shop. Then he popped his head back out. "Are you guys coming? I don't want you wandering off and leaving me lost in Lamu."

Matt laughed. "We're all here," he said, and followed him in.

Omari sat at a desk near the back of the shop holding a torch that spit out a bright blue flame. He aimed the flame at a silver ring he held with a pair of pliers. Then he took the ring and dropped it into a bowl of liquid on the desk. The ring hissed and sizzled for a second. He looked up. "How can I help you?" he asked. "Do you want to buy a silver necklace? A ring?"

He led us to his display case on the wall and pointed out the beautiful silver pieces.

"Actually," Dave said, "I met your cousin in Mombasa. He told me you might be able to teach me to be a silversmith."

Omari looked at Dave. "You want to be a silversmith? All four of you?"

"Oh, no," Matt said. "Just him."

Omari nodded. Then he led the way back to his workshop. Two teenage boys sat on stools, concentrating on their work. "I train people in the silversmith craft. I could give you a few lessons. Can you work hard?"

Dave nodded. "I've even done some metalwork." He explained about the rhino horn we had cast.

"Okay," Omari said. "If you come tomorrow morning I will teach you how to make silver rings."

"I'll be here," Dave said.

As we walked out of the shop and through the lengthening shadows to meet our dads for supper, Dave said, "I can't believe I'm going to learn how to be a silversmith."

THE LAMU
SILVERSMITH

The Olympic Restaurant was an open palm-thatched building on the waterfront. School chairs, painted blue, surrounded a few metal tables. We sat down and a cat immediately ran under the table and began rubbing my leg. I pushed it away and it went to Matt.

"Ahh!" he said jumping up. "I don't like cats rubbing my leg." He waved his arms and the cat scampered away.

"We have to try the lime milkshakes," my dad said, ordering a large one for each of us. Then we ordered fish and rice, each choosing his own kind of fish. I chose shark because I didn't like having to dodge fish bones. I'd learned in one of my books about the ocean that sharks have no bones, only cartilage.

"Shark!" Matt exclaimed. "Are you going to eat shark?"

He ordered kingfish. Others ordered tuna or red snapper. But I stuck with my decision to try shark.

Frosty glass mugs arrived first, filled to the brim with a green foamy liquid. I sucked up the lime shake in my straw. It was tart, yet with just enough sweetness. And cold! It cut through the thirst of a hot day better than a soda.

Matt sucked eagerly on his straw, too.

"This is great!" Dave said.

"Yeah," Jon agreed. "I could live on these!"

Matt merely nodded and kept drinking.

"Well, it's been quite a day, hasn't it?" Matt's dad said. "I still get shaky thinking about the holdup on the bus. God was really watching over us." Then he quoted 2 Timothy 4:18. "The Lord will rescue me from every evil attack and will bring me safely to his heavenly kingdom. To him be glory forever and ever. Amen."

"Does that mean that Christians will never be hurt?" Matt asked. "What about people who get hurt in accidents, or die of sickness?"

"A good question, Matt," his dad said. "It doesn't mean that Christians will never be hurt. Paul meant that nothing will happen that God doesn't allow. He will rescue us. There are times when he allows difficult things in our lives, even death, to test and strengthen our faith."

We sat quietly, thinking over what Matt's dad had said. Then Matt confessed, "I felt scared today. I thought we'd all die. But I have accepted Christ. Why should I be afraid?"

His dad put his arm around him. "We're all afraid of the unknown. Death scares all of us. I was scared today as well. We know that if we die we go to heaven yet we've never experienced it. So although we believe, we feel scared, and that's okay. I believe God will prepare us when the time comes."

Just then the food arrived. We dug into slabs of grilled fish seasoned with lemon and pepper and mounds of fried rice. It tasted delicious.

"How's your shark, Dean?" Matt teased.

"It's actually pretty good," I said giving him a small taste. He nodded approvingly. "And best of all," I added, "I don't have to worry about swallowing a fish bone."

The owner of the restaurant came over and asked how we liked our meal. We all agreed it was excellent. The man said his fishing boats brought in fresh fish every day.

He smiled and then made his way to greet another table of guests.

After supper we walked slowly along the waterfront, along with many of the townspeople. Men strolled in their white *kanzu* robes, while the women were completely covered in black *buibuis*. Young children ran and played tag. A few donkeys wandered untethered and undiapered. We watched the moon rise over the water where dhows bobbed gently on their anchors.

In our room Dave and I turned the fan on high, tucked in the mosquito nets and fell asleep.

The next morning we ate banana pancakes for breakfast and then went with Dave to the silversmith shop. Omari invited us in. "Today I will teach you how to make rings," he said. "First I will demonstrate." He took two thin pieces of silver wire. "I take the two pieces of wire and place them firmly in this vise." He put the other end of the double wires in the hole of a simple hand drill. "Then I turn the drill." The two wires began to twist into one.

"See how the wire is braided together. Now to make a ring." He formed the braided wire into a circle and cut the wire to make the correct size for the ring. "Next I will solder the ring to make the circle all one piece." He told Dave about his own special recipe for solder. Then he fired up his torch and heated the solder so it would form a strong weld. He worked so carefully we could hardly see where the two parts of the braided wire had been joined. Then he put the ring in a small bowl of water to cool it off.

Finally he placed the ring on a metal form that tapered like a finger. Omari pushed the ring down on the form the way you'd slip a ring on your finger. "This will make the ring completely round," he said.

He pulled the finished ring from the form and showed it to us. It looked beautiful. "Do you think I can do that?" Dave asked.

"That's why you're here," Omari said smiling. "But first, I want you to clean this ring." He took Dave back into the workshop and introduced him to the two young Swahili boys who were also apprentices. Giving Dave a small stool, Omari pointed out a large bowl with some seeds in the bottom.

"These seeds come from a tree that only grows on the coast," Omari said, taking some out and showing them to us. "They make an excellent lather that is just right for cleaning silver." He put his hand in the bowl and swished it around. Soon the bowl bubbled up as if someone had poured bubble bath under a running faucet.

"Put the ring in there and clean it," he told Dave and gave him a small brush to work with. "If the suds go down, take a handful of seeds and splash the water like I did. I will check your progress later. Then I will show you how we melt down silver and how to draw wire and make it thin."

We watched Dave for awhile. But the shop was small and we felt like we were in the way. Besides, how long can you watch a guy swishing up suds in a bowl and brushing a tiny ring?

"I'm bored," Matt announced. Dave looked hurt. "No, not with what you're doing, Dave. It's just that you're the only one who's doing it. We're just standing here. Maybe we'll go do something and come back and get you later."

We said good-bye and slipped out of the shop. We hadn't walked very far when someone grabbed Matt by the shoulder. "Do you boys want me to guide you around Lamu?" It was Ali. "I can arrange for a small fishing trip. Only fifty shillings each. You get to fish, then we will cook the fish along with rice over a campfire on Manda Island. You can swim. You can lay in the sand."

"Can we snorkel?" I asked, making motions to explain what I meant. "Oh, yes," Ali assured me.

"Let's go for it," Matt said.

"Yeah, I love fishing," Jon said. "But Ali, we don't have any fishing poles."

"You don't need any. We'll fish with lines that we throw over the side. Don't worry. We'll provide everything. Hooks and bait."

We went by our rooms to pick up towels, sunscreen and our snorkeling equipment. Then we went to the waterfront to meet Ali.

chapter eight

THE
SILVER
NECKLACE

On the way down to the jetty I announced, "I hope I find a *voluta lyraformis*."

"A what?" asked Matt. "What did you say you are looking for?"

"A *voluta lyraformis*," I said. "It's a kind of shell."

"A shell. I should have guessed. You always win first prize in the hobby show at school with your shell collection."

"It's a volute," I explained. "And it's shaped like a lyre, an old musical instrument kind of like a guitar. Whoever first discovered it called it the *voluta lyraformis*. The lyre-shaped volute. Anyway, it's a very rare shell and it's only found on the islands around Lamu. I saw one once that belonged to Mr. Senoff at school. He taught me about shells and has a beautiful volute. And he says he found it north of Lamu on a trip with a Bajuni fisherman. So I'm looking for one today."

"I just want to catch some fish," Jon said.

As we arrived at the waterfront we heard two men arguing violently. One of them was Ali. They were speaking Swahili even though it seemed to be faster and more slurred than what we were used to and words we'd never heard before. But Matt, our Swahili expert, could understand enough to tell us, "They're arguing over the price of renting the boat. Apparently he wants more than Ali told us it would cost."

Ali heard us talking and turned and gave us a tired smile. *"Hakuna matata,"* he said. "No problem. Just get in the boat. I'll run and get the needed supplies."

The boat's captain shouted what sounded like a curse.

Ali ignored him and ran off. We stood by the small sailboat, not sure whether to get in or not. But the captain smiled and invited us to climb on board.

Soon Ali returned with a bag full of things. Two young boys about our age came with him. Ali and the captain exchanged a few more words and came to an agreement about the price, and the captain set out.

It was only a short sail across the main channel from Lamu to Manda Island. Our captain steered the boat into some smaller channels fingering into the mangroves on Manda Island. "Here's where we can start fishing," Ali said, pulling out several wads of fishing line from his bag.

One of the two younger boys already had his line in his hand. He baited his hook and tossed his line out into the water. Within seconds he pulled in his line. A silver fish about the size of a pancake flapped back and forth on his hook. He pulled off the fish and baited his hook again.

Jon rushed over to Ali. "Give me a line and a hook," he said. "I want to catch some fish."

Ali showed him how to bait the hook. Jon's first attempt at throwing his line didn't go very far. It kind of plunked down into the water. Matt's first try was even worse. He swung his hook like David swinging his sling at Goliath. But Matt let go too soon and his hook went flying backwards into the sail. Everyone laughed as Matt had to climb up and unhook it.

But we soon got the hang of it. The fish we caught weren't big, but it was fun to feel the fish hit the hooks and then pull them in. Jon caught the most but Matt and I also caught three or four each.

I asked Ali about snorkeling. He talked to the captain and then told us to snorkel right there. Matt and Jon wanted to go on fishing. I put on my mask, adjusted the snorkel and jumped in. I couldn't find any coral growing there in the channels. I suspected it was out on the outer side of the island.

Swimming back to the boat I mentioned this to Ali. He shrugged. "The captain says you can snorkel here. He's not going farther." Even though Ali had gotten his way on the price for the day, the captain wasn't going to do any more than he had to for us.

I went back to snorkeling and managed to find a few different shells. I even swam over to the edge of Manda Island. I had to wade through black mud up to my knees to reach the mangroves. Then I examined the base of the slender roots of the plants. They were slimy, but I soon found what I was looking for — a black lumpy thing. I touched it and the fleshy covering revealed a glossy chocolate-brown shell. It was an onyx cowrie, a shell that grew well in mangrove swamps. I pocketed my treasure and swam slowly back to the boat. I kept a lookout for the *voluta lyraformis,* but didn't find one.

At the boat the fish had stopped biting. The captain pulled up anchor and sailed a short distance to where a beautiful white beach fronted the main channel. We were still within sight of Lamu town. The captain beached the boat and Ali and his two helpers ran ahead to start a fire. Soon they had a pot of rice bubbling and had cleaned and scaled our catch. They rubbed salt on the fish before roasting them over the fire. Ali told us to explore. "Takwa, the ruins of an old town, is on the other side of this island," he said. "I wanted to show you, but the captain says the tide is not right. But look around. Who knows what you might find. Food will be ready in half an hour."

We walked barefoot a short way over the sizzling sand. "Man, my feet are hot," said Matt, hopping into the shade of a bush. Then he really hopped around. "Ow! I stepped on a thorny vine," he shouted, hopping back onto the hot sand.

"Race you to the water," Jon said, changing our direction. We all ran, even Matt. The sand by the water was cooled by waves lapping the white sand. Matt sat down and picked the thorns out of his foot. None had gone in deep enough to do any serious damage.

As we sat with our feet in the water, I noticed a janthina floating by. I reached out and caught the beautiful purple snail shell.

"Is that your *voluta* whatever?" Matt asked.

"No, I couldn't find one," I said. "I told you they're rare. This is a janthina snail. It floats on the top of the ocean on this bubbly thing here that comes out of the shell." Matt and Jon reached over to feel the bubble on top.

"It feels like those packing bubbles," said Matt. "You know, the kind that come inside padded envelopes." We popped a few and a deep purple dye oozed out of the shell.

"I've got a lot of these in my collection," I said, "and I don't need another so I'll just toss it back."

As we watched it float along, Ali called that the food was ready. We walked over to the fire and sat down under the shade of a tree. Matt told Ali we prayed before a meal. They all nodded and kept silent while Matt prayed. "We pray too," Ali said. "Five times a day. We are good Muslims here on Lamu."

We ate the fish and rice. Despite the sand that somehow got into every bite, the meal tasted delicious.

Afterwards we all piled onto the boat for the ride home. As our captain headed down the channel, a much larger dhow sped across our path. Our captain pulled hard on his rudder to escape a collision. Standing, he shouted at the other boat to be careful. The dhow captain turned and yelled angrily that it was our fault and we should just get out of his way. I noticed that the dhow had a cargo of wooden boxes partially covered by torn canvas sheets. One of the sailors pulled on the canvas, trying to cover the boxes completely.

"He sure was rude," Matt said.

Ali agreed but didn't seem too upset by the man's outburst.

Back at the dock we thanked Ali, paid our money and

headed back to the Lamu Guest House. We saw Dave arriving at the same time.

"Hey, Dave," I called. "We thought you'd be there all day."

"Well, Omari sent me home a bit early," he answered.

"Why? Did you break something?" asked Matt, cheeky as usual.

"No," Dave said slowly, looking a bit puzzled. "But it was a strange ending to the day. Let's go have lime shakes and I'll tell you about it."

I threw my snorkeling gear into my room and we walked to the Olympic telling Dave about the boat trip, catching and eating fish. As we slurped on our drinks, Dave told us about his day. He unzipped his hip pack and pulled out five silver rings. Two were twisted double-wire rings. One had three wires braided. And the last two had been made with only one wire but they had a neat knot tied in the middle.

"Wow! Did you make all those, Dave?" I asked.

He nodded proudly. "And that's not all," he said. He reached into his hip pack and pulled out a fancy silver necklace. It had tiny little twists in it that made it look like the froth on the crest of a wave. "This is a filigree necklace," he said.

"It's beautiful," Matt said. "Did you make this too?"

"No, I didn't," Dave said. "But I know I could if I had enough practice. This necklace is a kind of a mystery, though. Three men came into the shop about an hour ago. One was much darker than the other two. One man looked like a Somali, and the third seemed to be an Arab. They came in and started arguing with Omari."

"What about?" Matt asked.

"I don't know. About the only words I could pick out

were some numbers. But they didn't make sense and I can't remember them now anyway. After a few minutes of arguing, Omari came back into the workshop. He slipped me this necklace and whispered that I should study it so he could show me how to make one like it tomorrow. I was surprised because this is much more difficult than the rings. Then Omari motioned for me to hide it in my hip pack and he told me to go home for the day.

"When I told him I wasn't finished, he grabbed my wrist and squeezed so hard it left a mark. See!" He showed us the red marks. "Then he said, 'Go now!' So I ran out of the shop. Before I got out the door, the three men started shouting at Omari again. I don't know what was going on, but they sure were angry."

chapter nine

THE
SILVERSMITH
DISAPPEARS

"It's a mystery, all right," Matt agreed, getting a closer look at the silver necklace.

He studied it and said, "I don't know if you could make a necklace like this, Dave. It would take ages."

"It looks really old to me," Jon announced, as he leaned over to see it better. "It's tarnished, almost like muddy sand marks."

"Well, we can't figure it out now," I said. "Maybe Omari will explain it to you tomorrow."

"I'm sure he will," Dave said. "Before those men showed up he was really nice. He even took me home for lunch. I

met his wife and young son. They live in an upstairs apartment farther back in town. Omari told me his favorite sport is soccer and he plays center halfback, just like I do. He said if we stayed until Saturday we could watch his team play."
We still had a lot of questions about Omari and the necklace, but it was getting late. We hurried back to meet our dads and Pastor Samuel.

After supper, we went to our rooms and played Uno under the slowly revolving ceiling fan. Soon I yawned. "I'm tired. Must be all the sunshine and swimming," I said.

"And the heat," Matt said, taking a towel and wiping the sweat streaming from his armpits. As he raised his arms he showed off his newly-sprouted armpit hair just to let us know he was growing up.

It wasn't the armpit hair that impressed Jon. "Phew! You stink, Matt!"

Matt took a sniff and wrinkled his nose. "Yeah, it is pretty bad, isn't it." He grinned.

"Well, I'm not spending the night with you unless you take a shower," said Jon.

"Don't worry," Matt said. "I'm going to take a shower and borrow some deodorant from my dad."

"Have you noticed how handy the shower is?" I asked. "The shower and the toilet are all in the same room."

"It is different than what we're used to," Dave said. "I'm just thankful they have showers. I'm after you, Matt."

The next morning after breakfast we walked with Dave to Omari's shop. The door was locked shut. We knocked but nobody answered. "Maybe we're early," I suggested. "You know how laid back things are here on the coast." So we sat in the shade and waited.

After half an hour, Matt stood up. "I don't know what's going on with Omari but it's obvious he's not coming in today. Let's go do something."

Dave looked sad. "Maybe I can try back later."

"I have an idea," I said. The other three looked at me. "We could go look at the Lamu Museum—"

"Museum!" Matt interrupted. "With all this sunshine you want to go to a museum?"

"Well," I began, defending my idea, "we passed the building several times walking along the waterfront. You know, the one with the cannons in front of it. I thought—"

"Cannons? Why didn't you say so?" Matt asked. "Let's go. I'll bet they have all kinds of weapons."

We checked out the cannons at the entrance before going in. The museum was an old Lamu house that had been restored. It was two stories tall with high ceilings to keep the place cool. Matt and Jon ran to all the displays of weapons — old swords and knives and things. There was even a display of bows and arrows from the Boni people, hunters who lived inland from Lamu.

"Look at this," Dave called. We looked at the display of the different kinds of dhows, most originally of Arabian design. "I didn't know there were so many kinds," Dave said. "I just called them all boats or dhows. The most common is the *mashua*. And look at the name of this kind. It's called a *jehazi*." We also looked at some carved round plaques from the front of dhows. They were said to be the eyes of the dhows with magical powers to ward off evil spirits.

"Seems like even the Muslims are afraid of evil spirits," I said.

We saw a room set up for a wedding in the old traditional

Lamu way. But the best display of all was the huge *siwa,* or horn, made of a giant elephant tusk. The *siwa* had been intricately carved and was considered a national treasure. Though it had been played in the past at special ceremonies, it now rested in a case in the museum.

"That's awesome," Dave said, admiring the craftsmanship.

"It sure is," Jon said. "I wonder where they found an elephant with tusks that size?"

As we moved out the door of the *siwa* room, Dave noticed silver jewelry on display. "Look at that necklace," Dave said. "It's almost identical to the one Omari gave me!"

I stepped over to look. "Are you sure?" I asked.

"Yeah," said Dave, pulling Omari's necklace out of his hip pack and holding it up. "A few of the Arabic letters are different. But otherwise, the two necklaces are alike."

He placed the necklace Omari had given him back in his hip pack. Leaning closer, he read the white note card. It explained that the necklace on display came from Pate Island to the north and was made during the 1600s at a time when the Sultans of Pate and Lamu were often at war. "That's interesting," he said.

"Yeah," I agreed. "But it doesn't tell us where Omari is or why he gave it to you."

"Maybe he'll be at his shop now," Dave said. We walked out of the cool museum into the hot sun. The silversmith's shop was still locked tight.

"Let's go swimming," Matt suggested. "For ten bob we can take a small dhow to Shela beach. It's where Lamu Island meets the Indian Ocean and Ali told me it's the only place to go body surfing."

We stopped by our rooms and grabbed our towels. On

the way to the waterfront we picked up some shish kebabs
and bought a couple of loaves of bread, a bag full of oranges,
and two bottles of Kilimanjaro bottled water. Then we caught
a boat to Shela beach. We weren't alone. A number of other
tourists lay there soaking in the sun. Most of the Lamu resi-
dents weren't too excited about all the visitors. I'd seen signs
telling guests not to walk around town in bathing suits. So
many of the tourists ended up on Shela beach for most of the
day.

We swam around in the warm Indian Ocean for a while
and tried to catch some waves. But the tide wasn't too great.
Soon we gave up and sat down in the sand.

A long-haired young man with a British accent asked Matt
where we came from. "You four look a bit young to be back-
packing across Africa."

When Matt told him we lived in Africa, the man, who
said his name was Scott, couldn't believe it. "You mean you
actually get to live here in Africa? All the time? Where do you
go to school?"

Matt explained about the school for missionary kids at
Rugendo. "Sounds grand," Scott said. "And you play rugby at
your school? I'm a rugby player myself." He pulled a small
rugby ball out of his backpack and asked if we wanted a
game of sand rugby. Matt's eyes widened with glee.

"Let me call some of my mates," Scott said. And soon we
had a game going. We were a lot smaller than the other guys,
but they only caught us and held us, instead of tackling us
hard. After the game we had to run into the ocean to wash off
the sand that stuck to our sweaty bodies.

Scott wanted to know what our parents did in Africa. So
we told him about my dad being an editor, Jon's dad being a

doctor, Dave's dad a builder and Matt's dad a Bible teacher. "Our parents are here to help people understand what it means to accept Jesus as their Savior and to learn how to follow Jesus."

Scott sat quietly. "I learned about Jesus when I was a boy about your age. But in high school and university I've been doing everything I can to forget him. I want to lead my own life."

I looked at Matt. Neither of us knew what to say. We knew people should follow Jesus, but we'd never really told people about Christ. That was something the grown-ups did. So we sat there and said nothing.

Scott looked up at the swimming pool blue sky. Then he turned to us. "You know what? You won't believe the mess I've made of my life. I can tell you one thing. I need to get right with God again. I leave Lamu tomorrow and I'm flying back to England next week. I'm going to go back and talk to my mum. I know she's been praying for me all these years. Thanks, boys, for showing me the way to go."

His friends were leaving so Scott said good-bye. We all looked at each other. "How did that happen?" Matt asked. "I think Scott began to believe in Jesus today and somehow we were part of it."

"It was his mom praying," Dave said.

"I can't wait to tell Dad," I said. "God used us, even though we didn't know what to say."

We ate our oranges and made meat sandwiches out of the shish kebabs and bread. Then we swam some more. The tide had gotten higher so, with the bigger waves, we got in some good body surfing.

Then we headed back to Lamu. "Let's stop by Omari's one

more time," Dave said. We knocked again, but the door remained firmly shut. I saw an old Arab man staring at us from a narrow alley beside the silversmith shop.

"I wonder if I should go to his home and see if he's there," Dave said. We went with him, but Omari's apartment was locked shut, too, and no one answered our loud knocking. "What am I supposed to do with this necklace?" Dave wondered. "I'm sure it's valuable. But if Omari's not at his shop and his wife's not home, what should I do with it?" None of us had an answer.

As we turned to walk down the spaghetti-thin lane, I saw the same Arab man. He stepped into the street blocking the way. "Why are you looking for Omari?" he asked in Swahili.

Dave answered, "He taught me how to make silver rings yesterday and I was supposed to come back for more lessons today. See." Dave stopped talking and opened his hip pack and showed the man the five rings he had crafted the day before.

"Well, Omari is not in," the man said.

"Do you know where he is?" Dave asked.

"No," the man said. "I don't know where he has gone. Maybe you should forget about learning from Omari."

"But I have a necklace that Omari gave me," Dave said. "I have to know how to get it back to him."

"Necklace?" the man asked, instantly alert. "What necklace?"

"This one," Dave said drawing the silver filigree jewelry from his hip pack.

The man's face took on a shocked look as he stared at it. His eyes opened as large as the dhow eyes we'd seen at the museum. Then he scuttled away down a dark alley, disappearing into the shadows.

chapter ten

A
THIEF
IN THE NIGHT

"I wonder who he was?" Matt asked.

"I don't know," said Dave. "He sure looked funny when he saw the necklace. I thought he might know a way to find Omari and get the necklace back to him. But now he's gone too."

We headed back to meet our dads at the guest house. As we got to the main street we heard shouting and saw a crowd of people. Young boys ran barefoot ahead of the mass of people that poured toward us like rain down a waterspout.

"What's going on?" I asked, almost in a panic.

"I don't know," said Matt, "but we'd better get out of the way."

We found a nook in the gray wall beside us and crowded into the small space. Soon the crowd streamed in front of us and stopped. I looked at Dave, my heart thumping. To our relief, they ignored us and began singing and dancing. Someone was beating a drum. One young man stood in the middle, a dazed smile on his face. The others cheered and flocked around him. A few minutes later, the crowd moved again, stopping about twenty yards up the road to sing again.

An African man had squeezed against the wall next to us. "What is this?" Matt asked him.

"It's a traditional Lamu wedding," the man answered. "The people celebrate like this. The young man in the middle is getting married."

"Why aren't you going with them?" Matt asked.

The man smiled. "I'm not from Lamu. I come from Kirinyaga. I'm just working here for Kenya Power and Light. I'm an engineer at the power generator at the far end of town. To these Muslims, I am an infidel, an unbeliever."

"We're from Rugendo," Matt said. "That's pretty close to Kirinyaga."

The man became excited and named some of his relatives from Rugendo. We knew a few of them from church.

The man said, "I am very lonely here. There are only a few other Christians. We meet in an old church dating from colonial times, but there are only a few of us from upcountry who attend. Most of the Muslims leave us out of everything." Then he smiled. "Greet my friends at Rugendo," he said. "And pray for me."

We found my dad waiting for us. "Did you see the

wedding procession?" he asked. We told him how we'd almost been run over in the stampede.

For supper we followed the signs to a restaurant called Ghai's. Ghai, the East Indian owner, told us how he'd left his high-paced job as a building contractor in Nairobi to run this restaurant in Lamu. We ordered prawn curry and mugs of freshly squeezed lime juice to quench the heat of the spicy food. As we ate we told our dads about meeting Scott on the beach. "He made a decision for the Lord right there," Matt said.

"That's great!" his dad said. "It's amazing how God brings people into our lives who are ready to follow Christ. Scott's heart was ready, even though you boys didn't know what to say. Just being there was enough."

Later my dad told stories about the wars between Lamu and Pate and how the Portuguese struggled to set one against the other and then take over. "Then when the British took over, Lamu had British government officials. Have you heard about the dugong in the British Museum in London?"

None of us had even heard of a dugong. "Well, it's kind of like a big walrus but without the tusks. It lives in the channels around Lamu and is often called a sea cow because it's a cousin to the manatee. The British Museum asked a government official to obtain a dugong skeleton. He had some of the local fishermen catch and kill a dugong. The official decided the quickest way to get the skeleton would be to leave the dugong in the water and let fish eat away the flesh. So they tied weights to the dugong's body and dropped it in the water. Right over there, I'm told," and he pointed.

We all looked out at the silver water of the harbor as it reflected the rising moon. My dad went on. "But they had a problem. The dugong's stomach gases had bloated the body and it refused to sink. The British officials realized they would have to puncture the stomach. So the men went out in a small boat to where the dugong's body floated." He stopped. "You boys have finished your supper, haven't you?"

We all nodded. He went on. "One of the men pierced the dugong's stomach with his sword. But when he did, a vile spray from the dugong's stomach contents spewed all over him."

"Gross!" Matt said. "That must have really stunk."

"It did," my dad said. "Then the officials decided to shoot the dugong. It hissed and finally sank beneath the surface. The men recovered the bones and the Lamu dugong skeleton is safely kept in the British Museum today."

We all laughed at the story. "Where do you get all these stories, Dad?" I asked.

"Various places," he answered. "I read the dugong account in a story by Edward Rodwell, a newspaper columnist who collects all kinds of stories about the coast. Some I get from reading old history books. Have you ever heard of the Pate Chronicle? It's an old book which claims to give a day-by-day history of the island of Pate which is north of Lamu. But judging by the stories in the Pate Chronicle, it's more likely fairy tale than truth. I've always wondered, though, about the mention of the lost town of Wale. It's referred to in the Pate Chronicle as a powerful town like Lamu, but no one has ever found a trace of it. Wale may be a myth or it may be called something else today, like Gedi. Or it could be a lost city waiting to be discovered..." His voice trailed off.

"Have you boys seen that hotel near the Lamu Museum?" he said, after a few moments of silence. "The one called

Petley's Inn? Well, the original owner of that hotel, Percy Petley, was one of the world's worst innkeepers. At mealtimes he would hold a loaf of bread against his bare chest, cut off hunks and throw them to guests across the table."

We all laughed. Ghai had walked up to our table with a big smile. "I trust your meal was better than those served by Percy Petley."

"Yes," Matt's dad said. "It was excellent."

On the way back to the guest house we asked my dad for advice about the silver necklace Dave still had stowed in his hip pack. "Omari disappeared?" my dad asked.

"We checked his shop three times and his house once," Dave said.

"I'm sure something came up and he had to go somewhere," Dad said. "Maybe he had to help with the wedding we saw today."

"But why didn't he tell me?" Dave asked.

"Here in Africa if someone doesn't come to an appointment, his absence tells the person waiting that the other one is not there," said Pastor Samuel. "Why tell him the obvious?"

"That's right," Dad said. "When you see Omari again, I'm sure he'll give you a reason why he was gone today. I suggest you go back to the shop tomorrow. If you haven't found him by then we'll figure out something to do with the necklace since we'll be leaving the next day."

That night was so hot that the fan couldn't stir up enough of a breeze to get cooler. I finally dozed off only to wake up drenched in sweat. As I woke up I turned. A moonbeam lit up a small square patch on the floor of the room. Then I saw a shadow move across the moonlit square!

A jolt of fear pierced my heart and I felt almost paralyzed.

A man dressed in white crept toward our window. One of the bars had been pulled out of the crumbling concrete and the man stepped out of our room.

"Dave!" I tried to call out but my voice got stuck. I tried to scream. This time my voice came out in a hoarse whisper. "Dave!" I said, finally finding my voice. "There was a man in our room!"

"What?" Dave asked groggily, turning over. I pointed at the window. "A man!" I said. "There was a man in our room."

Dave jumped up instantly, clawing his way out of the mosquito net. I followed him. We looked out the window and saw the back of a white robe flapping as the man disappeared across the rooftops.

Dave picked up the iron bar that had been uprooted from the window sill. "Stop!" he yelled. But the man didn't stop.

I ran to my dad's room. "Dad! Dad! Help! A man came into our room!"

All three men rushed out of their room. "Are you boys okay?" my dad asked, kneeling down by me. I nodded, but started to cry anyway.

"We're okay," Dave said, flipping on the light in our room. "But there was a man here. He pulled out one of the bars in the window sill and ran off over the rooftops."

Our dads looked at the bar. "You're sure neither of you is hurt?" my dad asked again.

"Just scared," I said. "I woke up and saw him climbing out the window."

"Let's pray and thank the Lord he didn't hurt you." With that my dad knelt down. Just then Matt and Jon stumbled into the room.

"What's going on?" Matt demanded.

My dad explained and we had a quick prayer of thanksgiving.

Matt's dad said, "I guess it was just a thief who got into the wrong room. You boys didn't have any money or cameras or anything else worth stealing."

Dave's face clouded over and he hurried to pick up his hip pack. The zipper was open. He looked inside before turning back to the rest of us. "It's gone!" he whispered. "The silver necklace has been stolen!"

chapter eleven

MISTAKEN IDENTITY!

"I'll bet it was that old man we saw outside of Omari's house today," said Matt.

"No, I don't think it was him," Dave said. "The thief ran like a much younger man. The old man outside Omari's house shuffled like a tortoise. But I do think he told someone we had the necklace, though. And that person stole it. The necklace must be pretty important."

Matt's dad peered into the night. "There's not much more we can do now," he said. "Whoever the thief was, he's long gone. We'll report it to the guest house manager in the morning."

"And I'll have to tell Omari the necklace is gone," Dave said with a sigh. "If we can find him, that is."

The next morning Matt's dad and my dad told the man who sat behind the desk at the guest house that someone had broken into the room. The manager looked shocked. He went up and looked at the iron bar that had been wrenched out of the window and said he would have it fixed. He also said he would report it to the police but doubted if they would catch the thief. He shook his head. "Stealing is really quite rare in Lamu. We Muslims have strict rules against it."

"So do we Christians," my dad said, "but that doesn't mean people don't steal."

The guest house manager nodded thoughtfully.

After breakfast Dave said, "I guess I'd better go tell Omari the necklace was stolen. If he's there."

We said good-bye to our dads and headed for the silver-smith's shop. The faded wooden doors remained shut, a rusty chain padlocked to the double wooden door handles.

Dave tugged on the chain in frustration. "I've got to find Omari," Dave said.

"I think Omari's disappearance has something to do with the necklace," Matt said. "After all, it must be valuable for someone to break in and steal it."

"Maybe Omari stole it back," I offered.

"Why would he do that?" Matt asked. "He gave it to Dave. All he has to do to get it back is ask Dave to give it to him."

I muttered, "It was just an idea."

"It's okay, Dean. We're all trying to figure out where Omari is and who stole the necklace," Dave said. "I just want some-one to tell me what's going on."

"Maybe the necklace was stolen from the museum," Jon suggested. "It looked a lot like that Pate necklace we saw, remember? And maybe Omari is in trouble for stealing it and—"

"I still think we need to find Omari," Dave repeated.

"You're right," Matt agreed. "But how? We've tried his shop. We've tried his house."

"Let's ask some people," Jon suggested, walking boldly into a nearby store that sold brightly colored cloth. He asked the shopkeeper where Omari had gone. The man, wearing his white Muslim skull cap and a pair of thick glasses pushed out on his nose, shook his head and said he had no idea.

We asked in another shop across the street from Omari's. But this man said abruptly that he didn't know and turned away.

"He doesn't even want to talk about Omari," said Matt.

"We're not getting anywhere asking people," Dave said. "They either don't know or they're too suspicious of strangers. Let's go check out Omari's apartment one more time."

Despite hammering on the door for a few minutes, we got no answer. A woman from the apartment below stepped outside of her apartment to shake her *mkeka*, a small reed rug. Matt called out and asked if she knew where Omari was. The woman quickly disappeared into her home without answering.

We walked slowly back down the street. Then we saw two older men resting on the stone bench, or *baraza*, outside their home. "I'm going to ask these guys," Dave said. "Excuse me, but do you know where Omari is?"

One of the men smiled and said he knew. And if we would follow him, he would lead us to Omari. We looked at each other with surprise and followed the man who leaned heavily on a wooden cane to help him walk.

We turned around one corner and the man motioned us to go into a leather-working shop. We walked in. It was dark with leather bags and sandals hanging everywhere. The old man said with pride, "This is my son, Omari. Do you want to buy some of his excellent shoes? A purse for your mother?"

We looked at the middle-aged man who stepped from behind the counter to greet us. "I am Omari, the shoe maker."

Dave said, "I'm sorry, we were looking for Omari the silversmith."

The old man looked blank. "I'm sorry, I don't know where the silversmith is," he said. "I thought you meant my son, Omari. Are you sure you don't want to buy some shoes?"

We apologized for wasting their time and backed out of the shop. "I give up," Matt said. "For a while I thought we were making progress. How were we to know there was more than one Omari in Lamu?"

"Actually, Omari is quite a common name," I said. "Kind of like asking for Smith or Jones in the States."

We walked quietly for a while. Then Dave said, "I just remembered a Bible verse my dad read in our family devotions before I came on this trip. It said, 'Cast all your cares on him for he cares for you.' I'm worried about Omari, but we've done about all we can do. So I'm going to pray and give it to God." Dave prayed quietly as we walked. I don't know about Jon and Matt, but I prayed too, asking God to help us find Omari and to keep him safe if anything bad had happened to him or his family.

"Well, this is our last day in Lamu," Matt said. "What do

you want to do? I don't want to waste the whole day." The blazing sun now lit up the shadowy streets.

"I'd like to find a shell dealer," I said, "to see if maybe he has one of those shells I'm looking for. The *voluta lyraformis*. I didn't have much luck out on the boat the other day."

We combed the shops that lined the street. One sold paintings and looked like a small art gallery. Most were crowded with bolts of cloth. In one fabric shop we saw a man sitting in the corner behind a foot-powered sewing machine, a worn and cracked yellow tape measure draped around his neck. His face wrinkled like used aluminum foil as he beamed a toothless grin at us. He motioned for us to come closer and offered to make a shirt for each of us from *khanga* cloth that hung from poles on the ceiling. We thanked him and told him we were looking for a shell dealer. He told us to check along the waterfront for the blue shell stand.

As we walked, a donkey loaded with mangoes in wide-mesh baskets forced us against the wall. We had to step into a gutter flowing with black stinky water. Matt looked down. "Look at this black crud all over my tennis shoes!" he said in disgust.

We all looked. Our shoes weren't any better. After the donkey passed we got back onto the street and tried to stamp the mucky slime off our shoes. Suddenly Dave bumped into me. "Watch what you're doing!" I said, struggling to catch my balance.

"Sorry," Dave answered. "Somebody shoved me from behind."

"Never mind," I said. "This street is so crowded. I know it wasn't your fault."

We walked on, stamping our feet. The smoke of roasting

shish kebabs filled the street and we couldn't pass by without buying some of the meat. But as Dave reached into his hip pack to pay for his shish kebab, he found it was already open.

"Oh, no!" Dave said. "My hip pack is unzipped!"

"So what?" asked Matt.

But I could see from Dave's eyes as he scrabbled his hand in the hip pack that something was wrong. "My wallet!" Dave exclaimed. "It's gone! Somebody's stolen it!"

He turned and started running down the narrow street. "Stop! Thief!" he called.

We followed Dave. A few people turned and watched us. But as fast as we ran, we couldn't find anyone suspicious.

"Looks like my wallet's gone," Dave said sadly. "I know I didn't have much money in it, but I made the wallet myself when we were in the States last summer."

Just then a tall man reached out and grabbed Dave by the shoulder. "Why are you running through our streets calling 'thief'?" he demanded.

"Someone stole my wallet," Dave explained. "Somebody bumped me and I think they must have unzipped my hip pack and slipped out my wallet."

"People in Lamu don't steal," the man said. "I own a shop and we do a lot of business with tourists. You must not run down the street yelling 'thief' when there is no thief. I don't want people thinking they will get robbed in the streets in Lamu."

"Well, my wallet is gone," said Dave. "If a thief didn't take it, where did it go?"

"Maybe it fell out of your hip pack," the man said.

"No," said Dave. "I always zip my hip pack."

"That's right," I agreed. "Dave never forgets things like that."

The man said again, very slowly, "I think it must have slipped out of your hip pack. Come, let us walk back toward where you came."

As we came near a small shop selling books and newspapers, the man stopped. "This is my store," he said. Then he pointed to the edge of the street. "What's that over there?" the man asked.

Dave walked over to see. Bending down he said happily, "Hey, this is my wallet." He opened it up. "And my money is still in it."

The man smiled. "I told you there was no thief. You must have just dropped it by mistake. And the good Muslims of Lamu are so honest that no one even picked it up."

"I'm glad to get my wallet back," Dave said, "but I know I didn't drop it. We weren't even on this side of the street. And there *are* thieves in Lamu. Last night someone broke into our room at the Lamu Guest House and stole a necklace from my hip pack."

The man's face clouded over in a fierce scowl and he retreated into his book shop.

Just then a young boy stuck his head around the corner from a tiny alley. Seeing us, he jumped like a frightened spring hare and ran away.

We started to move down the street when we heard a noise above us. We looked up and saw the wooden shutters of a second story window being pulled shut. All we could see were two thin fingers. Then the fingers disappeared as well.

chapter twelve

A NEW FRIEND

"Someone was up there watching us," Jon announced. We turned to ask the owner of the bookstore what was going on but the door to his shop was closed.

Dave frowned. "That's weird, man," he said. "I know my wallet didn't fall out. Someone stole it. But why did they put it back on the road? It seemed like that shopkeeper wanted us to find it."

"I give up. Let's just get out of here for now," Matt said. "Why would anyone steal your wallet and then put it back without taking the money? Fifty shillings isn't much, but I'll bet it's almost a day's wages around here."

"I'm getting hot and thirsty," Jon complained.

I looked ahead and saw a shop that sold cold drinks called a cold house. "Let's see what they have in there," I said.

We walked in and sat on the green metal chairs. A Pakistani man behind the counter asked what we wanted. "I make very good ices," he said, opening a massive chest freezer with rusty chunks flaking off the bottom. He displayed a multicolored popsicle. "Only two bob each," he said.

We each bought one. They were good and cold with a sharp fruit taste. "It's my own special recipe," the man said, smiling. "Mango, pineapple, lime, and tamarind."

"Really good," Matt said, forming the words around the popsicle that remained in his mouth. "I'll have another."

The popsicle man smiled and served up another round for each of us. "Where do you boys come from?" he asked. "I can tell you're not tourists."

We told him we lived at a place near Nairobi figuring no one in Lamu would have heard of Rugendo.

"I attended Aga Khan Academy in Nairobi. I have relatives there. Do you boys go to school there, too?"

"Actually," Matt answered for all of us, "we live at a place called Rugendo and attend a school for missionary children there."

The man became excited. "You're from Rugendo? My brother's life was saved there last year at the Rugendo Mission Hospital after a car crash. My brother and his wife were rushed to Rugendo where the American doctor took care of them."

Jon cut in, "That would have been my dad. He's the doctor at Rugendo."

"Your father was the doctor!" The man was really excited

now. "How can I repay you for what your father did? My brother had lost a lot of blood by the time he arrived at your hospital. Without a transfusion, he would have died. When he saw he had the same blood type as my brother, your father donated his own blood to save my brother's life. I know my brother thanked your father. But I have a chance to thank you, the doctor's son, on behalf of our family here in Lamu. I am so fortunate."

Jon looked a bit embarrassed. "I do remember my dad talking about people brought to the hospital after a car wreck last year. It must have been your brother."

"Yes, and we are so grateful. My name is Amin." He paused. "Here," he said, pulling out some more of his popsicles. "These are a gift from me. Now, I must get a gift for your father." He thought for a while. Then he nodded and smiled. "Come with me."

We followed Amin into the street. Soon he stopped at a big carved door. "Have you seen the beautiful doors in our city?"

We said we hadn't. As we followed Amin up and down the streets, he stopped at each of the richly carved doors. Some of the older ones had big brass spikes poking out. Some had been oiled and polished. Many were elephant gray with dry cracked wood. Most had carvings of leaves and other designs. "Lamu is famous for its doors," Amin said. "They are very valuable."

He stopped at a carpentry shop. The smell of freshly cut wood filled the room. "Some of our craftsmen still carve doors for tourists. That is okay. It's just not allowed to carry away the old doors from the buildings."

Amin went over to the carpenter and they began to have a

rapid discussion. In the end the man came over and gave Jon a beautifully carved two-piece Lamu chair. By sliding one piece into the other, they formed an X-shaped chair.

"This is for you to take back to your father," Amin said. "Try it."

They assembled the chair and we each took turns sitting in it. It was actually quite comfortable. Nodding happily, Amin asked the carpenter to take it apart and wrap it up for Jon. The carpenter's assistant wrapped the chair in heavy brown paper and then tied it tightly with rough sisal string. He even made a loop out of the longer length of string to make a handle.

Amin handed it to Jon. "For your father," he said simply.

Jon thanked him. As we walked back to Amin's cold house we passed Omari's silversmith shop. "Why isn't this door carved?" asked Dave.

Amin shrugged. "It was made recently. Why do you ask?"

"I spent a day with Omari," Dave said. "He was teaching me how to work silver into jewelry. Then he disappeared."

Amin tensed up like a cat ready to jump on a lizard. "Why are you concerned about Omari's disappearance?"

"He was my friend, for one thing," Dave said. "I know it's too late to learn any more about silversmithing from him since we're leaving tomorrow. But I'd like to say good-bye. And, most important, he gave me a necklace."

"He gave you a necklace? Made of silver?" Amin asked. Dave nodded.

Amin looked quickly up and down the street. "Come to my shop where we can talk without everyone listening."

At the cold house Amin sat down and looked intently at Dave. "Now, why would Omari give you a necklace?"

"He didn't give it to me, really," Dave said.

"What? You took it? Without permission?"

"No, of course not," Dave responded. "He gave it to me after three men came into the shop. He told me to go back to the guest house and study the necklace so I could make one like it. Then he pushed me out of the shop."

"Let me see the necklace," Amin said sharply.

"I can't," Dave said, looking miserable.

"Why not?"

"It was stolen last night. Someone broke into our room at the guest house and took it out of my hip pack," Dave explained.

Amin's eyes narrowed. "This is indeed a mystery," he said. "Can you describe what the necklace looked like?"

Dave sat up. "I can do better than that. I can show you one that is almost identical."

"Where?" Amin asked, surprised.

"In the museum," Dave said.

"Show me," Amin said, leading us to the museum. He paid for our entry fee and Dave walked ahead until he came to the display case with the ancient Pate silver necklace. "It looked just like that," Dave said.

Amin sucked in air with a hiss. "The legendary Wale necklace," he whispered. Then he looked straight at Dave. "You're sure the one was exactly like this?"

Dave nodded. Then he pointed at the small medallion. "Except for the writing on this coin-type of thing. It looked like Arabic letters but they were a bit different from this."

Amin looked upset. "You boys had better go. I don't think you'll find Omari."

"What do you mean?" Dave asked. "You know something you're not telling us!"

Amin's face hardened. "Just go. I can't tell you any more. Be thankful you no longer have the necklace." He stopped and looked around. A group of tourists came around the corner with a guide.

Amin motioned for us to move and he walked with us out of the museum. "Go now," he said. "Enjoy the rest of your last day in Lamu." Turning to Jon he went on, "Give your father the chair as a gift of thanks from me. With his blood flowing in my brother's veins, your father has become a true brother to me as well."

He looked around again, then finished in a harsh whisper, "As for the necklace, I suggest you forget you ever saw it. And stop searching for Omari." Then he turned and left.

chapter thirteen

MYSTERY
AT THE
FISH MARKET

We looked at each other. "What do you make of that?"
Matt asked.

"I don't know," Dave said. "One thing's for sure. He didn't
want us to keep looking for the necklace. What did he mean
calling it the Wale necklace?"

"Wasn't Wale that lost town your dad mentioned last
night?" Matt asked.

"Yeah," I answered. "Maybe he meant it came from Wale."

"But if the necklace came from Wale, that would mean
the town isn't lost anymore," Dave concluded. "Someone
must have found it!"

"And a silver necklace, too. I wonder if there's more treasure?" Matt asked.

"We should tell our dads," I said. "Maybe Omari is mixed up with a group of treasure robbers. It's illegal to take things from a ruined city. Amin was right. This thing is too big for us to handle."

"But where can we find them?" Jon asked. "They just told us to meet them at the Olympic this evening. They didn't tell us where they'd be during the day."

We sat down under a mango tree in silence, sweat beads trickling down our foreheads. Matt wiped his forehead with the back of his hand and said, "I can't think of much more we can do until we talk to our dads."

"Let's pray for Omari," Dave said. "It looks like he's doing something wrong. He was such a nice guy. I really don't think he's stealing treasure. But I do think he's in big trouble."

Just then a wavering cry broke through the air. We looked up, startled. The sound was coming from a mosque. "Just the Muslim call to prayer," Matt said, laughing. "It made me jump."

"Well, if the Muslims can pray now," Dave said, "so can we." As people hurried to the various mosques, we bowed our heads in the shade of the mango tree and asked God to protect Omari and give us wisdom.

When we finished, Matt said, "I just wish there was more we could do."

Dave said, "Praying was the best thing we could do. Now, why don't we help Dean find this shell dealer. Finding his guitar shell would be like finding a treasure."

"Yeah, let's go," I said. "And it's not a guitar shell. It's a lyre-shaped volute."

"Whatever," Dave said.

We walked down the waterfront until we found the shell shop. It was a small square wooden building with a rusty iron-sheet roof. A spider conch had been painted on the side to show it was a shell shop. Trays of shells were on display in the windows. Shark jaws dangled from a piece of sisal string.

"Look at those jaws!" Matt said with awe. He reached out to touch one. "Ouch!" he said, drawing back his finger which had a bright red spot of blood. "Those teeth are sharp! It sliced me."

An old man who'd been sleeping in a chair inside the shop sat up with a jerk and glared at us. Silvery white whiskers sprouted like cactus needles on his bronze face and his eyes looked bleary.

"What do you want?" he asked in a gruff voice.

"I was interested in buying a shell," I said timidly.

His face softened. Waving a hand over his trays of shells, he said, "Choose. I have many shells. Choose which one you want."

I was disappointed by the selection. All the shells in the trays looked faded and covered with dust. He had a few big murex shells and a passel of tiger cowries. But I already had those shells in my collection. I saw no *voluta lyraformis*.

The other guys were fascinated by the shark jaws. "Look how the teeth are layered on top of each other," Jon said. "Each tooth has four or five other teeth behind it, just ready to come to the front if one tooth gets broken off."

"Yeah," said Dave. "We only get two sets of teeth and have to use them for life. Sharks seem to have an unending supply."

"Well?" the dealer asked. "Which shell do you want?"

"Actually, I've been collecting for six years," I said. "I've found all these down near Mombasa. Don't you have any other shells?"

The man nodded. "So you're not just a tourist. You are a collector. Come in and I'll show you my specials."

Inside the shop the man motioned for me to sit on a stool. Then he reached under a stack of ragged newspapers and withdrew a brown envelope, soft and tattered from many openings. He opened it up to reveal some small cowrie shells. I looked at the jewel-like shells and then shook my head. "I have these, too." Picking up a beautiful specimen of the onyx cowrie I told him I'd found one just two days before in the mangroves. He nodded, but he could sense my disappointment.

"I do have one other shell," he said. "It's a volute that only comes from the islands around Lamu."

"The *voluta lyraformis?* You have one? Can I see it?"

The shell dealer smiled and pulled out another envelope, this time from a drawer hidden under the counter. Gently he pulled the shell out and put it in my hands. The rich brown and orange shell had finely cut ridges running up and down the length of its spiral shape. "It's awesome," I gasped. "Even more beautiful than in the pictures from my books."

The others stuck their heads in the window. "Did you find your shell, Dean?" Matt asked.

I showed them. "Hey, that is a good-looking shell," Dave said. "No wonder you collect those things."

"Well, buy it, Dean," Matt said. "I'm getting hungry. Seeing these shark jaws makes me want to sink my teeth into some food myself."

I turned to the shell dealer. "How much?" I asked.

"These shells are very difficult to find," the man said. "But I can see you want to own one and you are a true collector. For tourists, the price is two thousand shillings. For you, only one thousand shillings."

My stomach felt sick. I couldn't afford it. Not even at the local price. One thousand shillings was a good price. In the books the shell was valued at over seventy-five dollars and one thousand shillings was only about twenty-five dollars. But I didn't have nearly that much money. The shell dealer could see my face.

"I'm sorry," he said gently.

"Can you bring the price down?" I asked.

"No, that is already my lowest price. You see, these shells are very hard to find. In the past year, only two volute shells have been found in all of the Lamu area. Some years, the shells seem to increase and more are found. But not these days. The only shells found for the past year have come from the stomachs of a big fish we call the *tewa*. In English it is called a grouper. It lives in sea caves and it likes to eat the volute shells. Sometimes when the fishermen catch one they find these shells in the stomach of the fish. That is where this shell came from."

"Sounds a bit like Jesus telling Peter to catch a fish and take the coin out of its stomach to pay taxes," I said, laughing.

"Anyway," the man said, looking a bit puzzled by my story, "the fishermen sell the shells to me. They know the value and I have to pay them a lot of money. So I can't sell this shell for less than one thousand shillings."

"Well, maybe when I get more money I can come back

and buy one," I said. "But for now, I'm happy that I got a chance to see the *voluta lyraformis.*"

The dealer nodded. I looked around his shop and noticed a big murex, larger than any I'd ever seen. It was a fairly common shell but its size impressed me. "How much for that murex?" I asked.

The man smiled. "For you, a good friend, only five shillings. I pulled out a heavy silver five-shilling piece from my pocket and bought the murex which the man carefully wrapped in old newspaper to protect the shell's spines.

As we walked away, Matt said, "Too bad we didn't catch a grouper on our fishing trip. Maybe we could have found a volute in its stomach."

"That's a great idea!" I said.

"What?" asked Matt.

"Maybe we could buy one of those fish at the fish market. We could look inside and see if it swallowed a volute."

We looked at each other. "Yeah!" Matt said. "It's worth a try."

We hurried down the street to the warehouse-like building where fishermen brought their catch. We arrived at the time of day when the dealers had fish scattered along wooden tables.

As we stepped into the dingy building, we had to squint to see in the dim light. The stench of fish overpowered us. Matt said, "I don't know if I'm so hungry anymore. This place stinks!"

We went to one table and asked the man if he had a grouper. He didn't understand and tried to sell us a parrot fish. "Look at that guy's teeth," Jon said, examining the turquoise-blue fish. He touched the rock-like teeth that made the fish look like it had a parrot's beak.

"Those teeth are for eating coral," I said.

We told the man we didn't want a parrot fish. "What was the name that shell dealer used for a grouper?" I asked.

"*Tewa*," Matt said. "*Nani anauza tewa?* Who is selling grouper fish?" he asked.

The man pointed to a table farther back in the building. When we got there, the man told us he'd already sold all his catch for the day. Behind him we saw workers hastily putting fish into sacks.

"Please," I pleaded, "I only want one."

"There are plenty of other fish in the building," the fisher-man said.

"But I need a *tewa*," I explained.

Finally he agreed to sell me one small grouper. I paid him and waited for him to wrap the fish in old newspaper.

"Hey, look at what that guy's doing!" Matt said to the rest of us. "That guy, behind the table. Do you see him stuffing something into those fish before putting them in the sacks?"

We all tried to see. Even in the dim light we could see the glint of metal. The man seemed to be pulling things out of one box and stuffing them into the fish. As he reached into the box again, we could hear a heavy metallic rattle.

"What's he putting in those fish?" Matt asked, starting to walk behind the table.

Suddenly a man stood in front of Matt. "What are you boys doing here?" he demanded.

"Uh, just buying a fish," Matt said.

I recognized the man. "Matt, he's the captain who almost ran into us out in the channel."

The captain glared at us viciously. "Get out of here. Now!" He began pushing us out the door.

I barely had time to grab my fish before the man shoved us out into the sunlight and told us sharply not to come back.

chapter fourteen

TRAPPED!

We blinked in the bright sunshine. I clutched the grouper
with both hands. The wet fish had soaked through the newspaper and my hands smelled fishy. We walked quickly down
the street, buying shish kebabs and sugar cane on the way.
We sat on a bench near the Lamu fort and ate. "That guy did-
n't want us watching them pack those fish," I said. "What do
you think they were doing?"

Matt answered, "Something illegal, I'm sure. They were
stuffing some sort of metal into those fish. Do you think—"
He paused. "Do you think that might be this Wale treasure? I
mean, we saw that same captain carrying loaded boxes out of
one of the channels near here and he sure seemed annoyed at
anyone who got near him. Now we've seen some kind of

metal being stuffed into fish. Even if it's not silver treasure, it's still weird."

"I wish my dad was here. He'd know what to do," I said.

Dave spoke up, "Let's go talk to Amin again. He seemed to know something about the necklace that he wouldn't tell us. Maybe if we told him about the fish he'd know what to do."

"Better than sitting here," Matt said, standing up and leading the way back to Amin's cold house.

Amin smiled as we filed into his store. "You boys back for another popsicle?" he asked.

"We just saw something very strange at the fish market," Matt said, and he began to explain what happened when we bought the grouper fish.

Amin listened closely and asked a few questions. We all joined in with our answers. Amin nodded and said, "Yes, it makes sense. I think I know what to do. You boys stay here. Not all of those sailors are good people. Come into my office. You'll be safe here." He opened the door to a small office stacked high with receipts and order slips.

Once we stepped in, Amin swung the door shut and we heard an ominous click. Matt reached for the door handle and tugged. It refused to budge. "We're locked in," Matt said, slamming his fist against the door. "Hey, Amin, you don't have to lock us in."

But he got no answer. We could only hear the hum of the freezer in the room next door.

There were only two chairs in the office. Matt slumped into one. "Well, at least turn on the fan, Dean," he said irritably.

I did. We sat there not sure what to do. "I guess we'll have to wait," I said.

Matt stood up and paced back and forth like a caged lion. "How could we be so stupid to get ourselves locked up like this?" Matt demanded.

"Maybe we're losing our bush instincts after being in a town," Jon suggested.

"Amin did say we'd be safe here," Dave pointed out. "Maybe he locked the door to keep bad guys out."

"Maybe," Matt admitted, "but how do we know Amin's a good guy? We only met him this morning."

"He bought a gift for my father for saving his brother's life," Jon said.

"But what if it was all a trick to make us think he was our friend?" Matt asked. "What if he really wanted to see how much we knew about the stolen silver from the old ruins? When he realized we didn't know much this morning, he told us to forget it."

"He did look angry when he told us to forget about the silver necklace," I said, doubt beginning to form in my mind as well.

Matt went on, "Then when we came back and told him we figured out that the silver is being smuggled out of Lamu in fish, he locked us in this jail."

He stopped and looked around the room. It only had two windows, high on opposite walls. Metal bars set in concrete protected them.

"I'd better check our escape route," Matt said. "Dean, bring that chair over here and set it on top of this one. Now stand on the top chair," he told me. "Brace yourself against the wall," he said, and then clambered up the chairs and onto my shoulders. I began to teeter as he pulled his legs over my shoulders like he did when we had camel fights in the water.

"Hold still, Dean," he snapped.

"I'm trying," I said.

"Dave and Jon, you two guys come and hold Dean steady," Matt commanded. Then he started pushing on my head with his hands as he pushed himself higher. His shoes gouged into my shoulders.

"Careful, Matt, that hurts," I complained.

I heard him grunt and then felt another sharp pain in my shoulders as he dug his toes in and reached for the window. He gripped the iron bars and pulled himself up. I looked up and saw him dig his elbows into the small window sill. After a few moments he said, "Get steady, Dean. I'm coming down."

I leaned against the wall and soon felt Matt's feet kicking my ears as they groped for my shoulders. Then he slid down to the floor. "No way out there," he said. "The bars are solid. And besides, it looks like a fifteen foot drop from that window to the ground outside. Let's look out the other window."

We set up the chairs on the other wall and repeated the process. This time Matt discovered that the window stood only a few feet higher than the roof of a neighboring building. "We could easily walk onto that roof and get away," Matt said. "The only trouble is getting the bars off the window. He tucked himself into the narrow windowsill and asked us to give him some sort of tool to loosen the bars. Dave tossed him his Swiss army knife.

"Be careful with it," Dave said. "You'll probably do best using the saw blade. It's the thickest."

We stood under the window as Matt began gouging out

small chunks of concrete. Then he swept the concrete crumbs down on our heads so we all stepped back to keep the dust and chunks out of our eyes. After several minutes, Matt grunted.

"Making progress?" Dave asked.

"I've got a cramp in my leg," Matt said, shifting his position. "There, that's better. Anyway, I'm digging a small hole here, but the bar is a lot deeper into the wall than I thought." He jerked on the bar and it didn't budge. "I've got to keep trying," Matt said.

We stood back and continued to encourage Matt.

Then we heard voices. "Someone's coming," I whispered. "You'd better get down, Matt."

I scrambled up the chairs to help Matt get down. He eased himself onto my shoulders and the key in the door scraped. As I turned to see who was coming I felt Matt's foot slip on my shoulder.

"Don't move, Dean," Matt hissed. But it was too late. He began to fall. I tried to keep my balance, but the top chair toppled off and I crashed into a dusty pile of books. Matt landed on top of me.

We looked up to see Amin. Next to him stood Omari.

Matt stood up, dusting himself off. "Sorry about the mess," he said. "We weren't sure why you'd locked us up and were...well...trying to find a way out."

Amin shook his head in wonder. "It's no matter," he said. "What is important is that the men who were stealing the silver treasure of Wale have been stopped. And Omari and his family are safe."

Dave stepped over to Omari. "I'm glad you're safe," he said. "We prayed for you."

"Come, let's have a cold drink while we tell you what happened," Amin said.

We moved into his shop and he poured lime juice for everyone and began his story.

"There had been rumors for several months that some fishermen had found an ancient city. Many thought it was the legendary town of Wale. At one time there was a peace agreement between Lamu, Pate and Wale. A silversmith made three identical necklaces to symbolize the friendship of the three cities. The name of the city was written on each one. During a war that followed, the Sultan of Lamu melted down his necklace and had it made into a dagger to show that the peace had been broken. The Pate necklace is in the museum here. That's why when you said you'd found an identical necklace I knew it must have come from Wale."

"That's right," said Omari. "A few days ago, three men came to me with a silver necklace. They said they thought it was a forgery and wanted me to decide if it was the ancient necklace. When I examined it and read the inscription which said Wale, I knew it was the real thing. Some of the marks on the silver were exactly like the ones on the Pate necklace, made by a long-lost method of silverworking. But I suspected that these men were only interested in the money they could get. I realized they would sell everything they had found at Wale. I am only a poor silversmith. But I felt if I made a copy of the Wale necklace, I'd give the fake to the men and then hand the real one over to the museum. But they returned sooner than I expected. That's why I slipped the necklace to you, Dave."

"Why didn't you come back and get it?" Dave asked.

"After you left, I told the men I didn't have the necklace

with me. The men threatened me with death if I didn't give it to them the next morning. I still planned to get it from you in the evening and try my best to make a copy. But on my way home, I saw a man following me. I knew I would have to escape."

"How'd you get away? And where did you go?" asked Dave.

"I took my wife and baby son out our back window and across the rooftops to my friend's house — the man with the book shop. Then we waited for a chance to have one of his young cousins try to get the necklace back from you, Dave, without you knowing it."

"I knew my wallet was stolen that morning!" Dave said.

"Yes, it was us. But unfortunately, the necklace had already been stolen," Omari said. "My cousin grabbed your wallet hoping the necklace was hidden in it."

"I'm afraid that was our fault," said Dave. "I showed the necklace to an old man near your house who wanted to know why we were looking for you. He must have been a lookout for the treasure robbers."

"Once my friend the book shop owner heard that the necklace had been stolen the night before, we knew it was too late to recover it. We wanted to tell the police, but we had nothing to show them. And we knew these men were powerful. So I stayed hidden above my friend's shop."

"Was it you we saw closing the window?" Matt asked. Omari nodded.

Amin picked up the story. "When you said that Omari gave Dave a necklace just like the Pate necklace, I knew it must be the Wale silver. I knew my good friend Omari's disappearance must somehow be connected with the thieves.

The book shop owner told me he had Omari hidden. None of us knew what we could do to stop the thieves until you said you saw men putting some kind of metal into fish. I knew if we caught the thieves with the silver, they'd be arrested, but we had to work fast. Once fish are packed for export, the boats leave. Omari and I went to a customs official who is a member of our mosque. He alerted the customs department and they raided the fish market. The silver had been stuffed inside fish about to be cleared for export."

Omari smiled. "The men have been arrested and the silver has been recovered by the police. But I had a chance to look briefly at the treasure. Coins, jewelry, bracelets. It is filled with beautiful things. And, of course, the most precious find of all, the Wale necklace."

"The men will be forced to tell the location of the Wale ruins so the city can be excavated by archaeologists," said Amin. "It is so good knowing that the treasure of Wale has been saved thanks to you boys spotting the men hiding it in the fish."

"That reminds me," I said. "We never looked inside the grouper I bought to see if it had a volute inside!"

chapter fifteen

A RARE TREASURE

I reached under the table where I had put the fish when we had first come into the shop. "Do you have a knife?" I asked Amin.

Amin led the way back into the kitchen area of the store and pulled out a large knife. Everyone gathered around as I laid the fat grouper on a cutting board. With a big slice, I opened up the fish and pulled out the contents. Squiggly bits of fish insides covered the board. I reached around in the stomach and found nothing.

"No volute," I said sadly.

"Oh well, we tried," said Dave, trying to cheer me up.

"Besides, if you hadn't had your idea of buying this fish we wouldn't have caught the robbers."

Amin said, "We don't want good fish to go to waste. Why don't you boys invite your fathers and we'll have fish curry at my house tonight? Omari's family will come, too. Meet me here at the first hour of the evening and I'll show you to my home."

We waved good-bye and promised to join them for supper that evening.

Back at the guest house our dads had just returned. "We've had quite an adventure, Dad, and we're all invited out to supper," Matt said.

We decided to have one last lime milkshake at the Olympic as we waited to have supper at Amin's. At the restaurant we told how we'd been able to help catch the thieves who stole the silver treasure from the ruins of Wale.

"That's really exciting," my dad said. Then he led us in a prayer of thanksgiving to God for all of his help. "That's amazing how God answered your prayers," he said. "And I can't believe there really is a city of Wale. Maybe on another trip we'll be able to visit the ruins."

"How was your time down here at Lamu?" Matt asked his dad. "Do you have any ideas for telling the people here about Jesus?"

Mr. Chadwick looked serious. "It will be hard. The Muslims here are quite proud of their long tradition of Islam. They look down on African people as inferior. Many wouldn't even listen to Pastor Samuel."

Pastor Samuel went on, "There is a small church here, but it's mostly Africans. For now, the best thing to do is to pray for God to soften hearts. And perhaps one person could try to build friendships. Without actually showing God's love by our actions, nothing will happen."

"We made a friend," said Jon. "Or my dad did." He told of how friendly Amin had been after hearing it was Dr. Freedman who had saved Amin's brother.

My dad sat silently. "That's amazing. One act of kindness in central Kenya has reached down here and created a friendship, a starting point for sharing the gospel."

"Won't my dad be surprised?" Jon said.

"I wonder if he could do the same thing, only more often?" my dad said.

"What do you mean?" Mr. Chadwick asked. "I know God works in everything. But how often can Dr. Freedman expect to treat someone from Lamu at Rugendo?"

"Yes, but what if he came to Lamu? There is an airstrip on Manda Island. If he came once a month or so he could make a real contribution. Dr. Freedman could touch peoples' lives and create ways to share the Gospel."

He looked at us. "God has really used you boys this week in Lamu."

That evening my dad found out Amin was a member of the local Lion's Club, a group that often sponsored community projects. Amin was excited about the idea of Dr. Freedman coming to the hospital once a month and agreed to have his club help sponsor the trips. And we Rhinos especially enjoyed the fish curry and fresh bread.

"This fish sure tastes good," I said to my dad. "Too bad it didn't have a volute in it."

The next morning as we walked to the pier to catch the dhow ferry back to the bus stop at Mokowe, Dad told me to watch the bags and then he disappeared. I thought he'd walked away to get a better angle for a picture.

A few minutes later he touched me on the shoulder. "What do you think of this?" he asked, showing me a small package wrapped in newspaper. I looked puzzled.

"Come on," he said. "Open it up."

I did. "It's the *voluta lyraformis!*" I exclaimed. "Oh, Dad! Thanks! It's terrific!"

He smiled. "I thought you'd like it. It would have been a shame to go home without at least one treasure from Lamu."

"Thanks, Dad," I said and gave him a hug. "This has been a great trip."

He hugged me back. "Grab your bag," he said. "We've got a long safari before we get home."

THE END

GLOSSARY

1. *Turaco* (Too-ROCK-oh) — A large green bird that lives in the highland forests of Kenya. It has a dark blue crest on the top of its head. It makes a loud croaking call.

2. *Hoopoe* (HOOP-oh) — An orange-red bird with black-and-white wings. The hoopoe has a long slightly curved beak for eating bugs. It has a black-tipped crest on its head that often stands straight up.

3. *Bushbuck* — A small antelope that lives in forest thickets and dense bush. The bushbuck is mostly chestnut brown with white stripes and spots, about three feet high at the shoulder and has foot-long horns. It is shy and elusive, moving mostly at night. Its voice is a loud clear bark.

4. *Maasai* (MAW-sigh) — A tribe from East Africa. They are famous for keeping large herds of cattle and refusing to

change their traditional nomadic way of life. The women wear colorful beads while young warriors used to prove their manhood by killing a lion with a spear.

5. *Mosque* (Mawsk) — The building where Muslims worship Allah. Muslims wash and take off their shoes before entering a mosque. Many mosques in Mombasa have a loud-speaker system for the call to prayer which happens five times a day.

6. *Vervet monkey* (VER-vet) — A medium-sized monkey, part of the green monkey family. It has a dark face and white whiskers, and is light gray or olive green on the back with a white stomach. It has a long stiff tail and black feet.

7. *Topi* (TOH-pee) — A large chocolate-brown antelope with short, stubby horns. It has liver-colored patches on its face and shoulders. Topis often stand on anthills to watch out for lions and other predators.

8. *Dhow* (DOW [rhymes with cow]) — A wooden sailing ship of Arab design. Dhows have been used for 800 years or more to carry cargo between the East African coast and Arabia. Dhows come in many different sizes and many are still in use on the East African coast. Most dhows have a round wooden plaque painted near the bow or front of the ship. This "eye" is supposed to help the boat see where to go and to prevent misfortune.

9. *Volute* (Vuh-LOOT) — A family of shells. Volutes live in sand, and the snail inside the shell has a broad foot. Many volutes are brightly striped. The lyre-shaped volute in this story is rare and found only in Africa. It is about three inches long, peach-colored with brown and orange stripes.

10. *Janthina snail* (Jan-THEE-na) — A fragile shell that floats on the ocean surface in the tropics. It's about the size of

a half-dollar. The snail blows out a stream of sticky bubbles that help the shell float. When the snail is removed from the shell a dark purple dye oozes out.

11. *Onyx cowrie* (AWN-nix) — Cowries are a family of glossy rounded shells. The onyx cowrie looks much like the onyx stone from which it gets its name. The type of onyx cowrie found in East Africa is dark brown and usually found on mangroves in swampy areas along the coast.

12. *Dugong* (DOO-gong) — The dugong is related to the manatee from Florida. It looks like a walrus without tusks. A full-grown dugong can be ten feet long and weigh over 400 pounds. It lives in the ocean near shore and feeds on seaweed and other types of marine plants. Since it is a mammal it can only remain below water for five to ten minutes before surfacing to breathe through its nostrils.

13. *Murex* (MYOO-rex) — A family of spiny-armed shells. The Ramose Murex of the East African coast is white with a tinge of pink around the shell's mouth. The Ramose Murex can grow up to ten inches but the shells are normally about six inches long.

14. *Filigree* (FILL-uh-gree) — Ornamental work for various kinds of jewelry. It usually has an intricate design, often done with thin silver wire.